Touring Texas Gardens

Jessie Gunn Stephens

Republic of Texas Press
Plano, Texas

Library of Congress Cataloging-in-Publication Data

Stephens, Jessie Gunn.
Touring Texas gardens / Jessie Gunn Stephens.
p. cm.
ISBN 1-55622-934-8 (alk. paper)
1. Gardens—Texas—Guidebooks. 2. Texas–Guidebooks. I. Title.
SB466.U65 T477 2002
712'.09764—dc21 2002004159
CIP

Printed in the United States of America

Photos by author except where otherwise noted.

ISBN 1-55622-934-8
10 9 8 7 6 5 4 3 2 1
0206

All inquiries for volume purchases of this book should be addressed to Wordware Publishing, Inc., at 2320 Los Rios Boulevard, Plano, Texas 75074. Telephone inquiries may be made by calling:

(972) 423-0090

Contents

Part Three

Part Five

Part Six

Part One

Welcome to the Best-Kept Secret in Texas

"I must say as to what I have seen of Texas it is the garden spot of the world."

Davy Crockett, in his last extant letter, written on January 9, 1836

When you think of Texas, do you think of flowers? Yes, wildflowers, of course, bluebonnets and winecups and great swaths of prairie painted with bloom. But what about orchids? Or water lilies? Roses, herbs, ferns, and phlox?

They are all here in great profusion. And much else besides.

Welcome to one of the best-kept secrets in Texas—its wealth of beautiful public gardens.

Gardens are cultivated plantings. They are neither parks nor wildflower meadows, though you may find them inside parks, and many will incorporate native plants. Gardens demand gardeners, for someone must design them, plant them, weed them, water them, and feed them. It is the human hand that shapes them, and it is that shaping to which we respond because, while gardens reflect nature, they do so through a human mirror.

Unlike parks and other natural areas, gardens are usually not mandated by governments. Nor do they just happen, especially not in Texas. Almost always they arise from the dream of an individual or group of individuals sharing a vision, sometimes a pretty loony one, about creating beauty and order out of chaos. Those people have carved out magnificent gardens in the most unlikely of places and left legacies for the public to admire and enjoy. You'll find many of their stories—romantic, nostalgic, historically significant, or just plain colorful—in *Touring Texas Gardens*.

The element of surprise plays a major part in the charm of what you'll discover as you visit here. Much of the state's quarter-million square miles of land seems, and indeed is, inhospitable to gardens. The very unlikelihood of water lilies in San Angelo, irises in Abilene, or herbs in Fort Davis adds a special thrill to their discovery and raises questions about the people whose dreams made these wonders possible.

Few times in my life have I been more astonished than on the warm summer morning I drove through prairie grasses and mesquite thickets to discover Clark Gardens, a huge English estate garden atop a gentle hill near Mineral Wells.

"This just can't be here," I kept telling myself as I strolled the grounds. "It's impossible." Having grown up in exactly the same kind of country, I knew it was impossible. I felt as though I had somehow been snatched up from the rolling plains and plunked down in the English countryside, among sunken gardens, rose arbors, and black swans floating on dark pools of serenity. Once the shock began to wear off, I noticed something. While the effect of what I was seeing was that of a country estate in Britain, it was an illusion created almost entirely with plants native to Texas or with perennials, like daylilies and old garden roses, so perfectly adapted to the region that they had settled into permanent residence in local gardens a century and a half ago and so become "naturalized." The designers of this magnificent garden had taken the best of both the native and the traditional and adapted it to express their own vision of beauty. The rugged setting, which seemed at first to provide such contrast, became, when studied, the perfect framework for a thing of order and elegance.

That garden struck a chord in my spirit. It flooded my mind with images of my own pioneering forebears, farmers all, who first worked this unpromising land and learned to love it fiercely. It brought back memories of my grandmother's fragrant sweet peas and her petunias that never wilted in the sun, of her mother's moss rose seeds, hoarded and passed down the generations like heirlooms. It helped me remember who I am and why, just one in a long line of Texas gardeners and garden lovers.

Texas is full of surprises. That's why I call its gardens "the best-kept secret."

The Five Different States of Texas

"The sun has riz,
The sun has set,
And here we is
In Texas, yet."

A traveler's lament

When it comes to gardens, you can almost think of Texas as five different states, each of them larger than many states in the Union, and each presenting very different conditions for growing things. Gardens in far eastern Texas share little in common with gardens in far western reaches of the state. And Amarillo and Galveston might as well be on different planets.

Some experts on gardening go so far as to divide Texas into 10, 12, or even 19 separate regions, according to such factors as climate, soil conditions, rainfall, and wind.

Gardeners and farmers need that kind of detail. As tourists, we may content ourselves with dividing the state into a simpler jigsaw puzzle. Five pieces are all we need in order to talk about the public gardens of Texas—north, east, central, south, and west.

In the eastern and southern regions, you'll find gardens as lush and expansive as any in the nation. From the formalism of Houston's Bayou Bend, to the cottage gardens of the Antique Rose Emporium in Brenham, these areas offer a rich variety of garden experiences. In the north, the Dallas Arboretum and Botanic Garden provides year-round displays, while Fort Worth's Japanese Garden rivals any in the country.

Central Texas is home to herb gardens and perennial borders, as well as more formal plantings in botanical gardens and arboreta. The Lady Bird Johnson Wildflower Center in Austin forms an icon of design, architecture, water, and native plants.

And in the west—ah, the west—cacti and succulents and desert shrubs abound, of course, as do botanic gardens and rose gardens and lily gardens, in the last places you'd ever expect to find them.

Texas holds botanic treasures far beyond its much-publicized wildflower displays, including cultivated gardens for every season and every visitor—if you know where to find them. That's where this book comes in.

I am myself a travel-guide user. I rarely go anywhere without the latest edition of whatever guides are available to local bed and breakfasts, eateries, and tourist attractions.

I'm also a garden lover. Wherever I travel, and I travel extensively, I seek out the local gardens. In Texas, telephone books and chambers of commerce usually provide basic information to help me locate many of them. But the search is time-consuming and frustrating. No one source has known about all the gardens available for viewing at any one time, especially those at private homes that open to the public for only a few weeks in the spring or fall.

Until now, that is. Now I have *Touring Texas Gardens* tucked into my luggage, a guide that quickly and clearly provides all the information I need to plan visits to every region in the state, and so do you.

When to Visit Texas Gardens

"We ain't got but two seasons here—summer and January."

A Texas old-timer

In truth, gardens beckon visitors somewhere in Texas every season of the year, with the long spring and autumn seasons being especially inviting. The listings in the book will tell you when you may expect the most spectacular displays, as well as why you might want to visit a particular garden, even in the off-season.

We're a funny lot, we garden lovers. I once dragged my poor husband through Kew Gardens outside London in a cold drizzle in the middle of February. Why? Because it might be the only chance I ever got to visit this most famous of Old World gardens, and I was determined not to miss it. Little was in bloom, of course. In fact, most of the perennials weren't even visible, their tiny marker signs the only evidence that they lay sleeping beneath the soil. But I saw real yew hedges for the first time in my life. And black swans on the lake, and that glorious monstrosity of a conservatory they call the "Crystal Palace." It was an absolutely splendid day.

Like the English weather, so much has been written and so many jokes made about Texas weather that you might not need to read this section. But if your main impressions about Texas come second hand, take a moment to scan it. It will help you plan your visit.

The Garden in Winter

If you insist on flowers in the winter, concentrate on conservatories (gardens growing in the protection of glass houses), or confine your visits to the southernmost regions, where even a light frost is rare and flowers bloom year round.

But if your interests range beyond flowers, you'll find beauty enough in the winter gardens throughout the state. The bare trunks of ancient crape myrtles in Dallas, the splendor of towering pines in Nacogdoches, the irrepressibility of pansies in dozens of locations around the state fill the eye and draw the visitor even in dreary weather.

Japanese gardens capture the imagination as surely in winter as in any other season. This is when you can see the garden's structure most clearly and best grasp how evergreen elements blend with deciduous to create year long interest. Stonework, bamboo fences, tearooms, lanterns, rocks, and boulders reveal the true purpose of their careful placement.

And the winter garden lures birdwatchers. Now is when viewing conditions are ideal for spotting and identifying the shyer denizens of grove and glade. Over 600 species of birds have been sighted in Texas, and many of them make their winter homes in both rural and urban settings, especially where a rich variety of native plants offer shelter and food. Vermilion flycatchers overwinter in the Houston area,

rufous-sided towhees in Dallas. In El Paso, watch for the red-breasted nuthatch.

Spring in the Garden

Spring begins early in most regions. By early February, daffodils are beginning to brighten the woods of East Texas, and gardens everywhere are starting to color up with forsythia, Japanese quince, redbud, and dogwood. Azaleas and early-flowering perennials won't be far behind, followed quickly by roses. A vast array of flowers holds sway throughout the state in April, May, and June. Bluebonnets and other showy wildflowers have found a special place in cultivated gardens lately, and you'll see them in profusion.

Coping with the Texas Summer

Every part of Texas gets hot in the summer. Some smaller gardens may close their gates for six to eight weeks during July and August to let themselves and their plants have a break. Even the largest and best-maintained gardens may lose much of their spring luster during these weeks. Roses, including the ever-blooming types, take a rest, and only tough native perennials or constantly watered annuals keep gardens attractive. Many are, nonetheless, well worth a visit, even in the summer. Study the listings in the book, call ahead to ask what's worth seeing, and plot your excursions accordingly.

During the height of summer, plan your visits for as early in the day as possible. Wear loose, lightweight clothing and good walking shoes. Not all paths will be paved. Don't carry any more than you have to, but that might include sunglasses, sunblock, insect repellent, and a small container of drinking water.

If you're not acclimated to the heat, remember to move slowly. Set your pace according to the needs of the youngest or oldest members of your party. Gardens, after all, invite leisurely strolls. Take advantage of the opportunities they offer to take life easy for a while.

Except in desert regions, most Texas gardens are designed around large shade trees. You will particularly note (and appreciate) this fact if you visit during July and August when the sun is at its fiercest and humidity in some regions is high enough to fog up your sunglasses. In the best-designed gardens, shady walks meander beneath the leafy branches of huge native pecans, oaks, and elms, permitting visitors to view the sun-drenched planting beds without getting scorched themselves.

When you visit the deserts, shade may be offered only by man-made structures, and you'll have to seek it out, but you won't be having to cope with high humidity at the same time.

Wherever you are, substantial shade will usually be nearby. Look for it. Use it. Cool off. Rest. Often.

Another blessing in most parts of the state is a fairly constant refreshing breeze. Be aware of it, too, and use it to your advantage whenever possible. In other parts it can become a dehydrating factor, so don't let it dry you out.

Visitor centers and gift stores where present will be air conditioned. You can often seek momentary refuge in one of them.

The Blessings of Autumn

Fall is a time of renewal throughout much of the state, second only to spring in its boons. Temperatures drop, droughts end, and gardens refurbish themselves. Roses bloom. Wildflowers abound. The first frost holds off until early November, even in the Panhandle, until December on the Gulf Coast. In the Valley, it may not freeze at all. Everywhere, deciduous trees begin their blaze of glory. Pistachio, gingko, ash and oak, maple and gum put on a show, while chrysanthemums echo their colors at their feet.

What to Expect in Texas Gardens

"Texas should look like Texas, and Vermont like Vermont."

Lady Bird Johnson

Growing conditions in Texas are tough. They call for tough plants. But of course, tough is not enough. Gardens must be beautiful, too.

You won't find many delphiniums here, or dahlias, or any of the delicate darlings of the northern garden. If your concept of gardens admits nothing but wide expanses of green lawn flanked by clipped hedges and dotted with parterres or other formal plantings, you're going to have a short trip to Texas.

You will find a few of those, all right, especially in historic sites and large botanic gardens, but they form only a small percentage of what Texas has to offer. When you visit only these formal sites, you miss the delights of the desert, the hills, the scrub, and the river valleys, where lie some of the most intriguing gardens of all. That's where you'll discover just how beautiful "tough" can be, in the bounty of native and adapted plants and carefully maintained specialty gardens Texas is home to.

Native Plants

"The native flora of Texas is still among the most beautiful in all the world."

Benny J. Simpson, native plant pioneer

Native plants form the heart of some of the most successful gardens in Texas. In fact, part of the charm of such places lies in the skill and creativity with which designers have incorporated natives into their schemes. The beautifully exotic looking Asian gardens in Fort Worth, San Antonio, Houston, and Austin, for example, depend on natives to achieve many of their effects. And native pecan, elm, oak, cypress, magnolia, and pine trees make possible the very existence of others, providing a shady backbone around which to frame the planting beds we tend to think of as "the garden." That's why so many places you'll visit include the word "arboretum" (a place to preserve and study trees) in their titles.

Besides the native trees, many flowering shrubs and perennials that have graced the land forever untended now shine in planned gardens throughout the state.

That was not always the case. In the not-too-distant past, if Texas gardeners' interest in perennials went much past daylilies, irises, and other introduced species, they were likely to find few resources to which to turn, especially for native flora. The situation is very different now.

These days, a great deal of money and time are being expended by horticulturists trying to whip wildflowers into shape for use in the landscape. Breeding programs designed to produce smaller plants with bigger blooms and less invasive habits are common at universities and private greenhouses throughout the state. The result is a growing treasure house of blooming perennials and shrubs, bred from natives, but more manageable in controlled plantings.

Now you'll find azaleas, bluebonnets, salvias, hibiscus, columbines, cone flowers, daisies, penstemons, phloxes, rudbeckias, verbenas, and dozens of other natives among the ranks of blooming plants available in retail nurseries and on view in public gardens. You'll even find native herbs like bee balm and chile pequin, along with an ever-widening selection of ornamental grasses, shrubs, and trees. In fact, many public areas have come to depend on the tough beauty and tenacity of natives to inform the spirit of the whole garden. They can, for the most part, be maintained without synthetic fertilizers or toxic pest and disease controls, keeping the air free of harsh chemical smells. And all xeriscape (low-water usage) gardens depend on native plants.

Hardy Adapted Plants

Despite their reliance on natives, public gardens welcome introduced plants, once they have proven they can stand up to local conditions and perform. Annual beds, in particular, often fill up with colorful tropicals, showing off in the heat. Lantana, bougainvillea, and tropical hibiscus, not cold hardy in most parts of the state, are planted as annuals to brighten gardens throughout the summer. Impatiens, begonias, and caladiums join them in shady beds.

During colder months, pansies, dianthus, snapdragons, and other less-tender beauties bloom everywhere except the furthest northern and western reaches of the state.

Hardy, adapted perennials, such as Russian sage, scabiosa, rose, iris, narcissus, daylily, and foliage plants are grown throughout the state. In fact, some of them are so well adapted that entire gardens are dedicated to them.

Specialty Gardens

"Experiencing visual beauty depends upon our response to things sensed visually."

Jules Janick, Perdue University
or, as someone once said,

"Beauty lies in the eye of the beholder."

Though cacti have never held much appeal for me, I know people who collect and grow them with great fondness. Others are mad about irises, orchids, daylilies, ferns, water lilies, or roses. Gardens showcasing such specialty interests abound in Texas. So do thematic plantings, celebrating a motif, like butterflies, fragrance, or medicinal usage. You'll find herb gardens and organic gardens and gardens dedicated to romance, meditation, or a single color, wildflower plantings, cutting gardens, wetlands, and conservatories full of tropical plants. Whatever your special gardening interest, the chances are good you'll find a place where it's being expressed by others who share your passion.

What the Gardens Expect of You

"Gardens need and deserve the respect of all who visit them. They can't exist without it."

Anonymous groundskeeper, 2001

The main thing to remember about visiting gardens is that they are not parks. They require a different set of rules of etiquette. Created to preserve and display beauty, gardens should be treated more like museums, less like playgrounds.

In fact, while many gardens seem park-like, with expanses of lawn or other open areas, their purpose is very different from a park's, and in most you will be expected to leave your Frisbees and balls in the car.

Flowers delight us all, of course. And while one daisy beheaded by curious fingers won't seriously injure a planting, systematic picking (or whacking with a stick or tromping through) most certainly will. The garden is a "look, don't touch" experience for everyone.

Please teach your children to stay on marked paths, off the trees, and out of the flowerbeds. If you want to take their picture, pose them in front of the flowers, not inside a bed.

Water features are forms of art, not wading pools.

Wildlife, like butterflies, caterpillars, toads, squirrels, and other creatures, make their homes in the garden. They have as much right to remain undisturbed there as your family has to be left alone in your own home.

Be aware, too, that pets may not be welcome in some gardens. If you're traveling with pets, make some accommodation for them that doesn't include leaving them inside a closed vehicle. Ambient temperatures can reach the 100s even in early spring in some areas, creating dangerous conditions very quickly in cars or vans.

Visiting Gardens on Private Property

Some of the loveliest gardens grow on private property. They are open during certain days of the year only through the graciousness of the private citizens who own them, and only at their owners' discretion. Such sites will be marked, "Private, please call for information," in the listings. Please treat these residences as you would the home of any stranger, making sure your visit will be welcome by calling the number in the listing before setting out.

If You Live and Garden in Texas

"What with Indian raids, droughts, Santa Anna, the Civil War, and assorted other bothersome situations, early Texans had precious little time to think about gardening for pleasure."

Sally Wasowski, *Native Texas Plants*

Time is still a precious commodity, but today gardening for pleasure is a lot more doable, as the shrub borders, perennial beds, lawns, and vegetable plots around private homes testify all over the state. Texans love to garden. And we get some of our best ideas by visiting the public gardens in our areas. There's where we see the newest plants being tested for use in the landscape and get reacquainted with the tried and true stalwarts; where we learn what to plant in the shade, what will lure butterflies, which perennials will truly survive under our growing conditions, and what blooms even in the heat of the summer. Visit your public gardens, and support them, too. They are some of your very best resources for successful gardening in the state of Texas.

Making the Most of Your Guidebook

Sections of the book are devoted to each of the five regions we've divided the state into. Gardens are listed within the regions alphabetically, according to the nearest town or city. If you're looking for a particular garden by name, the index at the back of the book will guide you to its listing. You can also use Appendix D to locate gardens of a particular type, such as Japanese, English, or butterfly garden.

Within the listing for each garden, you'll find the information you need for planning your visit, including hours of operation, accessibility, and special features you won't want to miss. Have fun, and welcome to Texas.

"What sport shall we devise here in this garden,
to drive away the heavy thought of care?"

William Shakespeare

Part Two

The Gardens of North Texas

Dallas, Ennis, Fort Worth, McKinney, Paris, Sherman, Waco, Weatherford, Whitewright

The countryside in the North Central region of Texas is mostly savanna and prairie, with soils ranging from almost black to near white and browns and reds in between. Rainfall varies across the region from about 45 inches a year in the east to no more than 30 in the west. In winter, temperatures in the north can dip to 10 degrees Fahrenheit, in the south to 15. Summers are hot all over the area, with mean maximum temperatures in July hovering in the upper 90s and 100 degree days not uncommon.

Most gardens will be open year round, though activity at the smaller sites may well slow down (or stop altogether) during the coldest and hottest times of the year. April, May, June, September, and October provide optimal experiences everywhere in the region.

In years of normal rainfall, some kind of native flower is showing off along this region's highways from late February through mid-November.

In the spring, wildflowers can be spectacular on state and local highways, though bluebonnets (the state flower) will be found only where the Texas Department of Transportation has planted them, usually on sharply sloping embankments along the road. Spring-blooming flowers native to the area include coreopsis, both purple and yellow coneflowers, blue-eyed grass, bee balm, standing cypress, and prairie verbena. Attention-grabbing non-natives blooming at this time include crimson clover and purple vetch.

Wildflower production during the summer depends heavily on rainfall. Normally, common sunflowers, ironweed, black-eyed Susan, Texas thistle, partridge pea, verbenas, and blue salvias bloom through the hottest months.

Come September, a completely different complement of native blooms brightens the roadsides, with gay feather, asters, goldenrod, Mexican sage, and Maximillian sunflower stealing the show.

You'll find these and many other native flowers integrated into planned landscapes in almost every garden you visit. That's one of the ways they manage to have something in bloom nine months out of the year.

One of the major pleasures of driving through Texas is the birdlife visible and active along the roadways. In this region, you'll start up eastern meadowlark along country roads, glimpse belted kingfisher perched on branches or wires over creeks and marshes, and maybe race a roadrunner down a fence line. Other highly visible roadside birds include red-tailed hawk, northern harrier, American kestrel, northern mockingbird, eastern bluebird, and great blue heron all year, plus barn swallow, scissor-tailed flycatcher, and eastern and western flycatcher in summer.

Gardens, parks, nature trails, and a National Wildlife Refuge offer abundant birding opportunities. If you are using a national bird identification guide, you will need the Eastern version for this region.

Dallas

Dallas Arboretum

8525 Garland Road
Dallas, Texas 75218
214-327-8263
214-327-4901 Event Hotline
http://wwwdallasarboretum.org

Fee: Adults $6; Seniors 65+ $5; Children 3-12 years $3; Children 2 and under free; members free. Parking $3.

Accessibility: Excellent throughout the grounds. Wheelchairs are available at the front gate on a first-come basis, and volunteers run comfortable motorized trams throughout the grounds (except in January and February).

Days and Hours: Open every day except Thanksgiving, Christmas, and New Year's Days, 10-5.

Special hours: June, July, and August, the garden stays open until 9:00 on Thursdays for live musical performances and is open 8:00 A.M. till 6:00 P.M. on weekends.

Garden type: Arboretum, botanical garden, devoted to research and education, as well as to public display.

Garden size: Sixty-six acres; plan a full day here in spring or fall, at least three hours in summer or winter. Bring your camera.

Themes and Special Features: Dedicated gardens for azaleas, camellias, ferns, roses, white flowers, four-season annual flowers, and culinary herbs. The oldest tree in the Arboretum—a 200-year-old pecan. A magnificent southern magnolia allee planted in 1940. Bronze sculptures of Texas wildlife and other artwork throughout the grounds. Ingenious and handsome water features. A Woman's Garden with reflecting pool. A trial garden for testing newly introduced plants for adaptability to local growing conditions. Restored historic gardens.

The Garden: "Big D" is a city that likes to think itself sophisticated, even cosmopolitan, with its world-class high-rises and sports complexes, its restaurants and high-tech industries. This garden helps to legitimate that claim. Built on the grounds of two historic estates overlooking lovely White Rock Lake, it's truly a four-season delight and deserves a visit no matter what time of year you happen to be in Dallas. If January is particularly dreadful, the pansies and other winter-blooming annuals may suffer, but they will quickly spring back or be replaced. And while lesser gardens languish in August heat, here native perennials and annuals from the tropics keep the planting beds ablaze with color.

The estate houses around which the plantings lie are the white brick Camp House and the 21,000-square-foot DeGolyer home, built in 1940 in the Spanish colonial revival style. Mrs. DeGolyer's extensive gardens remain true to the period, including a sunken feature and several striking sculptures.

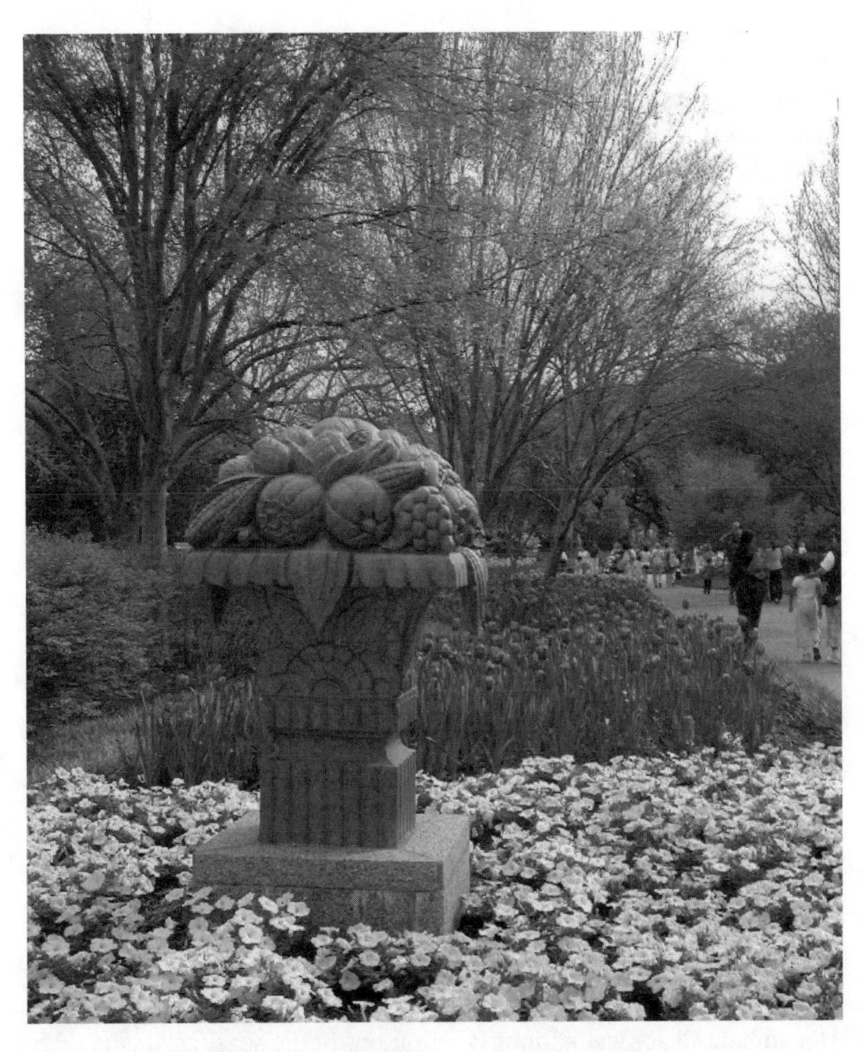

"Texas Pioneer Adventure" is a two-acre exhibit featuring a sod house surrounded by vegetable and cottage gardens, looking very much as they would have in the 19th century.

What's in Bloom: From late winter through April, look for a succession of blooms, starting with jasmine in A Woman's Garden, and followed quickly by dogwood, redbud, azalea, flowering fruit trees, and bulbs. Roses begin blooming in April and will continue to put on a show until the weather really warms up, then again in autumn. Summer-blooming perennials and annuals for both sun and shade keep interest high throughout the grounds, to be supplanted by later bloomers in the fall. Camellias highlight the early winter garden, backed by ferns and other evergreens, and pansies and white narcissus will bloom well before Christmas.

Don't-Miss Feature: You will love Toad Corner, an ingenious and enchanting water feature, located at the end of an allee of old, smooth-trunked crape myrtles on the far eastern side of the grounds. Also, look for life-like bronze sculptures of Texas wildlife placed artfully throughout the Lay Ornamental Garden to surprise and delight.

Bird Alert: Blue-gray gnatcatcher, Carolina chickadee, Carolina wren, downy woodpecker, northern mockingbird, red-bellied woodpecker, ruby-throated hummingbird, scissor-tailed flycatcher, tufted titmouse all appear here. Over 200 species of birds have been recorded in the vicinity of White Rock Lake, and the varied terrain, with both open spaces and wooded areas, encourages a variety within the Arboretum's grounds. This is especially true during the winter months, when an American white pelican or a great blue heron might soar by. Check the leafless trees for warblers like orange-crowned and yellow-rumped, as well as the tiny kinglets, golden-crowned and ruby-crowned.

Sponsored activities: Three special events held every year attract thousands of visitors: "Dallas Blooms," in the spring, "Dallas Blooms Harvest of Cultures" in the fall, and "Holiday at the Arboretum" in December. All are weeks-long celebrations of the seasons, designed to show off the gardens at their best and to provide special entertainment for the whole family.

An extensive schedule of special and educational events also keeps visitors flocking in year round. School bus parking is free, and groups of school children glory in both freeform and guided tours designed to teach life sciences and respect for the natural world.

Lecture and workshop programs for adults take place from January through May, family entertainments throughout the summer.

To learn more about the educational programs, either children's or adult's, call 214-328-4556.

Tours and Rentals: Several of the loveliest and most historic sites within the garden are available for weddings and receptions at reasonable, though not modest, fees. So popular are they that a special bridal hotline has been set up. Call 214-320-1268 for information. Rentals are available for corporate meetings and other functions, too. Call 214-327-8263 for information or send email to KREARDON@dallasarboretum.org.

Volunteer and Support Opportunities: The Dallas Arboretum and Botanical Society plans, develops, and manages the property. They invite all visitors to become involved. Memberships in the Dallas Arboretum range from "Individual" to "Friend," at varying levels of donation. Memberships at all levels include year-round admission and parking, with no waiting in line at the entry gate during major events, discounts on workshops and gift-store purchases, and a quarterly newsletter.

Donations of any size are always welcome, from individuals or corporations, and arrangements can be made to sponsor events, dedicate memorials, or assign honorariums and tributes.

Driving instructions: From IH-635 on the north side of the Metroplex, take Garland Road south about five miles. Watch for the Arboretum on your right. Or from IH-30 East near downtown Dallas, exit at Barry/East Grand. Cross Barry on the service road, and turn left (north) onto East Grand Avenue, which becomes Garland Road. The Arboretum is on your left, about three miles up.

Texas Discovery Gardens and Conservatory

3601 Martin Luther King Jr. Boulevard
P.O. Box 152537
Dallas, Texas 75315
214-428-7476

Located inside the Texas State Fair grounds. See Driving Instructions below.

Fee: Free.

Accessibility: Excellent.

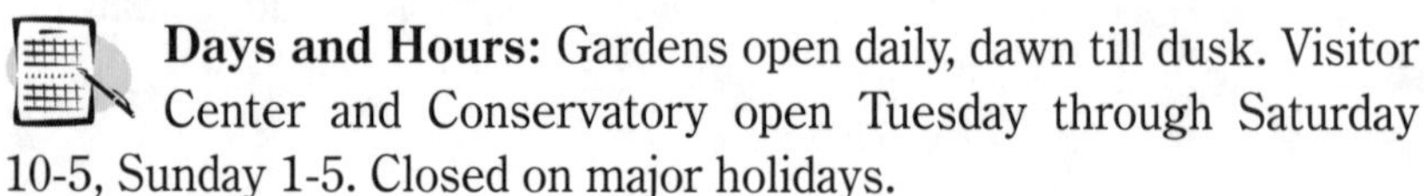

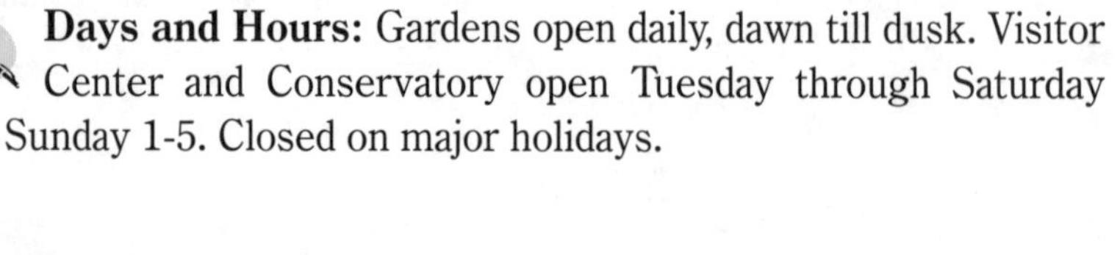

Days and Hours: Gardens open daily, dawn till dusk. Visitor Center and Conservatory open Tuesday through Saturday 10-5, Sunday 1-5. Closed on major holidays.

Garden Type: Arboretum and display garden, designed to showcase native plants in an urban environment and teach the conservation of nature. Tropical conservatory doubles during the State Fair as a living butterfly exhibit.

Garden Size: About seven and a half acres.

Themes and Special Features: Highlights include a Formal Rose Garden, All-America Selections Display Garden, Benny Simpson Native Plant Collection (over 250 species), Composting Exhibit, and Certified Butterfly Habitat Garden.

The folks here are serious about butterflies. They see them as a kind of easy-to-access interface between nature and people who don't know much about nature. The beauty of butterflies, as well as of many of the plants that sustain them, works magic on visitors young and old, as they learn about the relationship between themselves and butterflies, bugs and botany.

Once a year, during the annual State Fair, the garden's conservatory becomes an indoor butterfly haven, through a special permit issued by the U.S. Department of Agriculture for the importing and holding of exotic butterflies. Within the conservatory's protection, thousands of butterflies undergo their wondrous life cycles, to the delight of the visiting public.

Outside, all summer long, wild butterflies swarm over the display Butterfly Garden, which has been planted with carefully selected varieties that local and migrating butterflies rely on. You can get mobbed by feeding butterflies here, as they flit from penta to aster to lantana to cashmere bouquet to Mexican milkweed to salvia and daisy.

The Gardens: Almost all gardens that feature native plants proclaim their intent to educate the public about the use of low-maintenance, low-water-usage native and adapted plants in the home landscape. This garden fulfills that mission better than many. It shows that you don't have to turn your yard into a cottage garden to capitalize on low-maintenance plants.

You will stroll along smooth pathways lined with orderly edging plants and formally clipped hedges, not unlike those favored by many local homeowners. A reflecting pool, modern artwork, clever landscaping, and sophisticated bed design await you. A Portuguese cypress grows side by side with Texas star hibiscus, both grounded by a mix of red, pink, and purple natives, with those colors echoed and expanded by a mix of annuals.

Although you will encounter native and adapted plants throughout the grounds, the cottage-garden look is strictly reserved for the Heirloom Garden, Butterfly Garden, and Test Garden. Even there, a sense of order reigns, and you can see the spirit that informs this place in its tidiness. Here, you really can get the sense of how these plants would look in your own urban yard.

Then, of course, there's the grand allee, a planting of hollies over azaleas, that leads up to a huge formal water feature and color planting at the far end of the garden. Not too many homeowners will be looking to reproduce that effect, but we can all enjoy the serene beauty it creates.

Don't-Miss Feature: The shapers of this garden have made generous use of one of my favorite plants, the butterfly bush, in several colors throughout the grounds. Watch for the one with spires of rich, glistening purple so dark it seems almost black. That one is called black knight, and people find it as irresistible as the butterflies do.

Bird Alert: Year-round residents here include Carolina chickadee, northern cardinal, and northern mockingbird. In summer they are joined by ruby-throated hummingbird.

Sponsored Activities: A strong program of educational workshops goes on all year here, with particular emphasis on youth education, since a "hook 'em on nature while they're young" philosophy has been a driving force here since the 1960s. Events are presented both on site and in area classrooms. Adult and teacher education programs offer advice on everything from growing perennials to participating in national environmental programs, like Project WILD. Plans are in place for a continual expansion of outreach programs to students, senior citizens, and community organizations.

A Community Gardens program is already working with communities to turn vacant properties into gardens, while increasing neighborhood communication and cohesion. And botanical and ecological exhibits throughout the year educate the public in the Visitor Center.

Sunday afternoons in July offer a special treat, as the gardens host free concerts in their Basically Beethoven series.

Tour and Rental Policies: Self-guided tours are available at any time. To arrange a more formal tour, call 214-428-7476. If you are looking for a splendid venue for a business meeting, formal party, or wedding, call 214-428-7476.

Volunteer and Support Opportunities: If you want to get involved in growing things in the Dallas area, boy, do these folks have a job for you. Over 140 volunteers are needed during the State Fair Butterfly Exhibit alone, and as a mostly self-supporting nonprofit institution, the gardens depend on the help of nature-loving volunteers. The staff stands poised to offer the training you'll need to work in the greenhouse, lead tours and give programs, or just pass out brochures to visitors. You choose the level of involvement, and they will welcome you on board.

Driving Instructions: Texas Discovery Gardens lies inside the grounds of Fair Park, which is on the east side of downtown Dallas, just south of IH-30. I'm going to give you detailed driving instructions, but if you have trouble finding the park, just follow the signs pointing to the State Fair, the Cotton Bowl, or the IMAX Theater. They will lead you onto the grounds, and you can look for signs directing you to the gardens.

From IH-30 East, take the Second Avenue exit, curve to the right, and turn left at the second light, which is Martin Luther King Jr. Boulevard.

From IH-30 West, take the First Avenue exit, turn under the freeway to Exposition Avenue, and turn right on Parry Avenue. Turn left at the fourth light, which is Martin Luther King Jr. Boulevard.

From IH-45 South, take the Martin Luther King Jr. Boulevard exit, curve to the right, and turn left at the traffic signal.

Signs will tell you when you have arrived at Texas Discovery Gardens. Park immediately inside the fair grounds, in one of the lots along Second Avenue, and walk across the street. The Garden Visitor Center is the first building on your right.

June Delights: Dallas Area AHS Display Gardens

During two weekends in late spring every year, the Daylily Growers of Dallas open several private gardens so that the public may view the key American Hemerocallis display gardens. Some of them are listed below. Call for dates and directions.

Amerson Daylily Garden, 972-241-1726
Hillcrest Iris and Daylily Gardens, 214-352-2191
Hurst Park Daylily Garden, 817-268-5189

Ennis

State Bluebonnet Trail

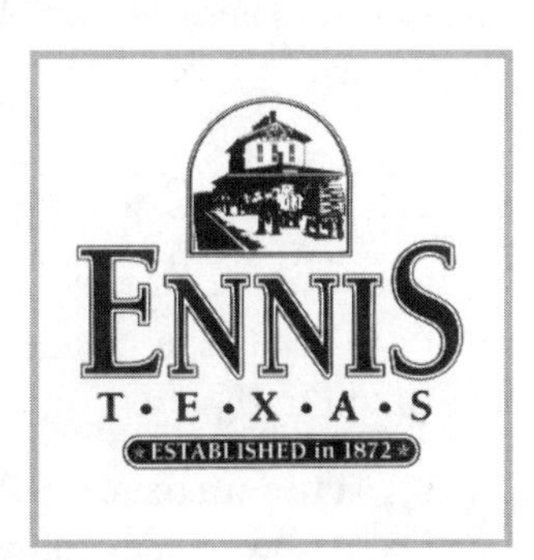

Ennis Convention and Visitor Bureau
002 East Ennis Avenue
Ennis, Texas 75119
888-366-4748
email: ennis4u@swbell.net
http://www.visitennis.org

 **Fee:** Free.

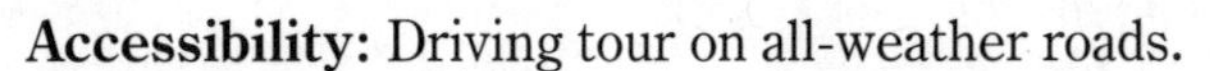

Accessibility: Driving tour on all-weather roads.

 **Days and Hours:** Daylight hours throughout the month of April.

Garden Type: Mapped driving trail to view bluebonnets and other wildflowers.

Garden Size: More than 40 miles on the map. Pick up your map at the Ennis Convention and Visitors Bureau on West Ennis Street downtown.

Themes and Special Features: Sponsored by the Ennis Garden Club, this is the oldest bluebonnet trail in the state and the legislature-designated Official Texas Bluebonnet Trail. Thousands of people turn out for these celebrations, so plan ahead if you expect to stay overnight in the area.

The Gardens: Blue is the keynote, with fiery accents of orange and yellow. Roadsides are blanketed with the color show that Texas is famous for.

Bird Alert: In April you should see dicksissels perched on fence posts along the pasture wires, singing their heads off, and eastern bluebirds chasing insects to feed their young. Eastern and western kingbirds will put in an appearance, too. The graceful swoopers you see near bridges and underpasses are probably barn swallows.

Sponsored Activities: One weekend will be set aside for a street festival. Call for this year's dates.

Tour Policy: Tours are self-guided, aided by an excellent map.

Driving Instructions: From IH-45, take exit 253 or 251B. Or from U.S. Highway 287, exit at U.S. Business 287 in Ennis. Head downtown to the Convention and Visitor Bureau to grab a map, and follow it into bluebonnet territory.

Fort Worth

Fort Worth Botanic Garden

3220 Botanic Garden Boulevard
Fort Worth, Texas 76107
817-871-7686; Conservatory 817-871-7689
http://www.fortworthgov.org/pacs/botgarden

Fee: Free to the grounds. Very small admission to the Conservatory.

Accessibility: Good.

Days and Hours: Open 10-9 Monday through Friday, 10-6 Saturday, 1-6 Sunday. Conservatory hours vary. Call 817-871-7689 for up-to-date information.

Garden Type: A true botanic garden, begun in the early 1930s and still dedicated to the display of a wide diversity of plant species, both native and exotic.

Garden Size: One hundred nine wooded acres in the heart of Fort Worth's near west side. The Conservatory is 10,000 square feet. Pick up a free map at the visitor center. You can cruise between widely separated sections of the garden by automobile.

Themes and Special Features: About two dozen specialty gardens mean something interesting going on here year round. The Japanese Garden (see below) and tropical conservatory provide winter interest, while layouts featuring cacti, roses, fragrant plants, and blooming perennials brighten the other months.

The Gardens: This wonderful garden boasts many delights and at least two of them are world-class—the Oval Rose Garden with its splendid rose ramp and the Japanese Garden (which I have given an entry of its own following this one). But to get the full effect of this, the oldest botanical garden in the state, start your tour at the newest part, the handsome Garden Center. You will soon see that age confers grace to this garden, not fuddy-duddyism. Pause to admire plantings of modern design adorned with artwork and water features before you even enter the building. Inside, you will want to pick up a map of the entire grounds and, for a small fee, tour the conservatory's impressive collection of tropical plants, including orchids and bromeliads. Behind the center, the Leonard Courtyard and Fuller Garden extend the mix of modern and traditional, with arbors of native vines, lavenders growing in the shade, perennials of every color and texture, and some of the most interesting garden hardscape you will find anywhere, including stacked stone walls, footbridges, fountains, and statuary.

Foot trails will lead you to the rest of the garden from here, or you may retrieve your car from the parking lot in front of the Garden Center and drive to the southwest sections. You don't have to go back out onto University Drive to do this. Just follow the signs through the park-like grounds.

The Japanese Garden will appear on your right and the Rose Garden on your left. Park at either.

You won't see much of the Rose Garden until you're almost upon it. It sweeps down from the crest of a gentle height into a valley of glorious color. This ramp of roses leads to the formal Oval Rose Garden, a marvel to behold in full bloom, as it is in spring and autumn, and worth visiting during any of the warmer months. More than 3,400 roses bloom in these gardens.

A path leading off to your left will take you to the Republic of Texas Rose Garden, featuring heritage roses that would have been available in the 1830s and 1840s, during the ten years Texas was a republic. To see the largest number of plants bloom in this garden, come in April, since many of these older roses are not reliably reblooming. The historic interest, of course, is seasonless.

Don't-Miss Feature: It may seem strange to focus on a restaurant as a don't-miss feature of a garden, and I haven't done so anywhere else, but I would be remiss not to tell you about The Gardens Restaurant within the park on Rock Springs Road. You have to pass by it, anyway, if you want to visit the Fragrance Garden, so why not take a peek at the day's menu? A favorite lunch venue for the old-money set I call "garden ladies who lunch," still, it's family friendly and offers some of the best cuisine in the city at reasonable, if not cheap prices. The Sunday brunch buffet is especially delectable. The restaurant's number is 817-731-2547.

Bird Alert: Across University Drive from the Botanical Garden lies Trinity Park, named for the river that flows through it. This has to be one of the oldest municipal parks in the state, because I remember playing here as a child and it was old then. Today it still welcomes joggers and picnickers and families looking for a shady spot to spend a summer afternoon, so while the trees here are ancient and huge, they don't harbor as many species of birds as they would in a quieter area. But red-bellied and downy woodpeckers live in the garden, as do mourning dove and brown thrasher. Certainly, tufted titmouse and Carolina chickadee can be seen or at least heard almost any time of year. Blue jays and northern cardinals can look like flowers on bare winter branches. The summer hummingbird will be ruby-throated or perhaps black-chinned.

Sponsored Activities: Special events in the gardens and the visitor center are scheduled throughout the year. An annual celebration of butterflies brings in not only thousands of butterflies to the conservatory, but educational opportunities for all. Call for up-to-date information.

Tour and Rental Policies: Self-guided tours are a pleasure here, with map in hand. Docents are available to serve as guides with adequate advance notice. Be sure to call well ahead at 817-871-7606.

Rooms for meetings and other functions are available, and very nice rooms they are, too, in the Garden Center. A plush auditorium seats 241, with one of the rear gardens serving as an outdoor break area. Smaller rooms are also available, and weddings can be hosted at various sites throughout the grounds. To learn more about reserving the facilities, call 817-871-7673.

The Japanese Garden offers even more opportunities for rentals, including a pavilion with a commercial-type kitchen where caterers can set up to serve your group.

Gift Shop: The well-stocked Treasure Tree Gift Shop is located in the Japanese Garden.

Volunteer and Support Opportunities: The Fort Worth Botanical Society helps support and sustain the gardens, which are part of the Fort Worth Parks and Community Services Department. Membership in the Society brings free admission to the Japanese Garden and conservatory, discounts, newsletters, and special members-only events. You can get an application by calling 817-871-7686.

Driving Instructions: Going east on IH-30, take the exit for University Drive North, circle under the freeway, and head down University.

If you're going west on IH-30, take the University Drive exit and turn left at the traffic light.

Once you are on University Drive going north, the first garden entrance you see on the left leads to the Japanese Garden, Rose Garden, and The Gardens Restaurant. If you want to begin your tour at the

Visitor Center, keep going and watch for another entrance (also on the left) just beyond.

Japanese Garden in Fort Worth Botanic Garden

3220 Botanic Boulevard
Fort Worth, Texas 76107
817-871-7685

Fee: Adults $2 Monday-Friday; $2.50 Saturday and Sunday; Seniors $.50 less; Children 4-12 $1.

Accessibility: Good.

Days and Hours: April-October 9-7 daily; November-March 10-4 daily.

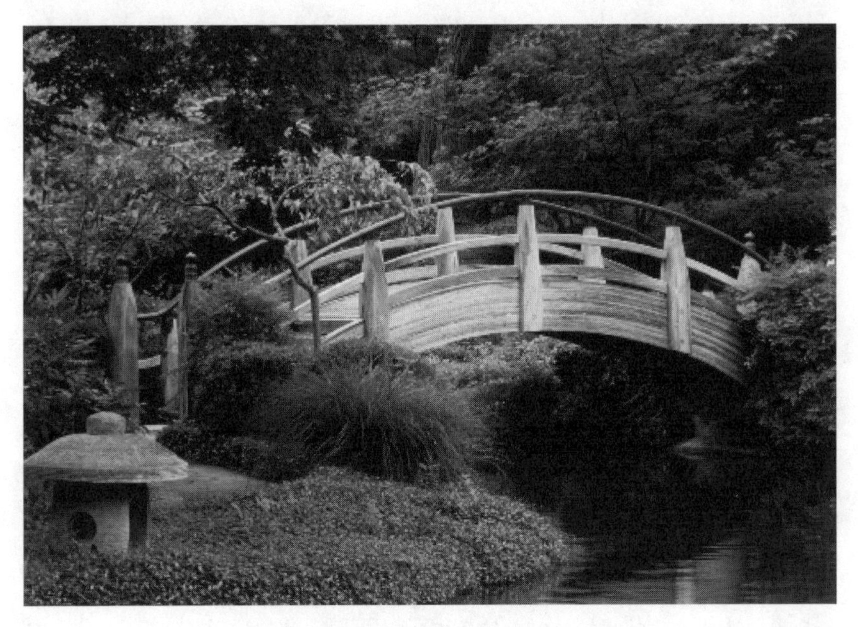

Photo courtesy Fort Worth Botanic Garden

Garden Type: Authentic Japanese-style stroll garden, incorporating many plants native to the area.

Garden Size: Just over seven acres.

Themes and Special Features: The main gate, which dominates the view from the parking lot, was designed by Fort Worth architect Albert Komatsu. It sets the stage dramatically for the intense experience that awaits you within the walls of this exquisite garden. Come at a time when you can bring quiet with you, or at least at a time when, given the opportunity, you can find it within yourself. The opportunity lies here.

The Gardens: It seems almost trite to praise a Japanese garden for the sense of harmony or relaxed solitude it invokes, but tranquility really is the keynote of this place. Bright color is a feature for only short flings in early spring and late fall, first when the azaleas blaze and then when the maples prepare to shed their finery for the winter. Texture, shadow, shape, and suggestion provide the garden experience. Rock is as important as plant. Water and walkway, pagoda and teahouse, all meld into one expression of calm beauty.

Don't-Miss Feature: Koi lurk in the pond, some magnificent specimens, too, and turtles, as well.

Bird Alert: You will hear the calls of native birds here, Carolina chickadee and a wren, perhaps. Mourning doves lend a note of pining to the air in the cooler parts of the day.

Sponsored Activities: October brings festival time, when all things Japanese are celebrated. Dance, martial arts, and the gentle arts of bonsai, ikebana, origami, and calligraphy are often featured. This may be your opportunity to learn about the true tea ceremony.

Gift Shop: The Treasure Tree strikes a nice balance between educational and decorative, with books and games for children and adults, as well as beautiful nature-related gift items.

Tour and Rental Policies: Tours are self-guided. A large pavilion, with amenities necessary for catering parties, is

available for rental, and it affords an absolutely stunning setting for a wedding, anniversary, or corporate event.

Volunteer and Support Opportunities: The Fort Worth Botanical Society helps Fort Worth Parks and Community Services Department support and sustain the garden. Membership in the Society brings free admission to the Japanese Garden and conservatory, discounts, newsletters, and special members-only events. Call 817-870-7686 for an application.

Driving Instructions: Going east on IH-30, take the exit for University Drive North, circle under the freeway, and head down University.

If you're going west on IH-30, take the University Drive exit and turn left at the traffic light.

Once you are on University Drive going north, start looking to your left for the entrance to the Botanic Gardens. This is a busy street and you're going to make a left turn across traffic. If you miss the turn, you can go on a little to the Garden Center, turn left there, and wind back through the park to the Japanese Garden, or else start your tour at the Center.

If you are coming from the parking lot of the Botanic Garden Center, look for the signs and follow them through the park (take the car if it's a hot day) toward the Japanese Garden.

Weston Gardens in Bloom

8101 Anglin Drive
Fort Worth, Texas 76140
817-572-0549
email: weston@westongardens.com
http://www.westongardens.com

Fee: Free

Accessibility: Good to variable.

Days and Hours: From mid-February through October, open 9-6 Monday through Saturday and noon-5 on Sunday. From November until mid-February, open Monday through Saturday 9-5.

Garden Type: Retail nursery and display garden featuring English-style mixed borders, old roses, and native plants.

Organic Policies: Encourages the use of less toxic and more natural organic products to maintain the garden.

Garden Size: About four acres in the gardens, seven for the nursery.

Photo courtesy Weston Gardens

Themes and Special Features: Since the English mixed border sets the style here, you won't find much in the way of clipped hedges or formally tended beds. Most of the plants are native or familiar adapted perennials like Russian sage and old roses, used in the naturalistic mode so prevalent in England. They tend to spread and sprawl a bit, looking for sun where there's too much shade, reseeding happily, and welcoming the sparrows and other birds that scratch among them.

Built on the grounds of an estate abandoned in the 1930s, with old crumbling brick buildings forming a backdrop, this place exudes a lovely romantic aura. The feeling of the garden is old, nostalgic even, but not grandmotherly or cottagey. On even the brightest days, red rock remnants of aged structures loom from thick shadows along trails lined with shade-loving shrubs and ground covers.

The Gardens: Sue and Randy Weston bought the grounds on which the gardens lie in 1988 and began excavating and restoring the estate's original hardscape, including a brick lily pond and a limestone arbor. Restoring the garden's original plantings was not part

Photo courtesy Weston Gardens

of the plan, though. The Westons wanted a place to show their customers how to use native and adapted perennials in their home landscapes. Now, water gardens complete with koi compete for the visitor's attention with roses in bloom and shady fern beds, as well as colorful natives like purple coneflower and red, white, pink, and blue salvias.

The gardens display their finest apparel from April through June and then again in October. At the end of the spring selling season, many busy nurseries like this one carry an air of exhaustion into the hottest part of the summer. They need to rest up a bit before the cooler weather revives them in the fall.

Bird Alert: Blue jay, Carolina chickadee, tufted titmouse, and northern mockingbird can all turn up in the woods that surround this garden. The unique sounds of wrens and woodpeckers often fill the air.

Sponsored Activities: The nursery sponsors workshops and seminars regularly for its many visitors and customers. Call for a current schedule.

Tour Policy: Tours are self-guided.

Gift Shop and Retail Store: Determined to sell only plants that have proven their ability to thrive under local conditions, the Westons have developed a valuable resource for Texas gardeners. Here is where I bought my first native penstemons, tall verbenas, ox-eye daisies, and blue mist flowers a decade ago. Their descendants still bloom happily for me in my North Central Texas landscape.

The shop offers a good assortment of garden decor, water features, books, seeds, tools, and trinkets, besides an unrivaled selection of Texas native perennials, ornamental grasses, trees, and shrubs. You will find antique roses here, too, in great profusion, as well as plants for xeriscaping. Another valuable offering you'll find in the store is a collection of very informative free handouts about planting and caring for perennials, roses, and other adapted plants.

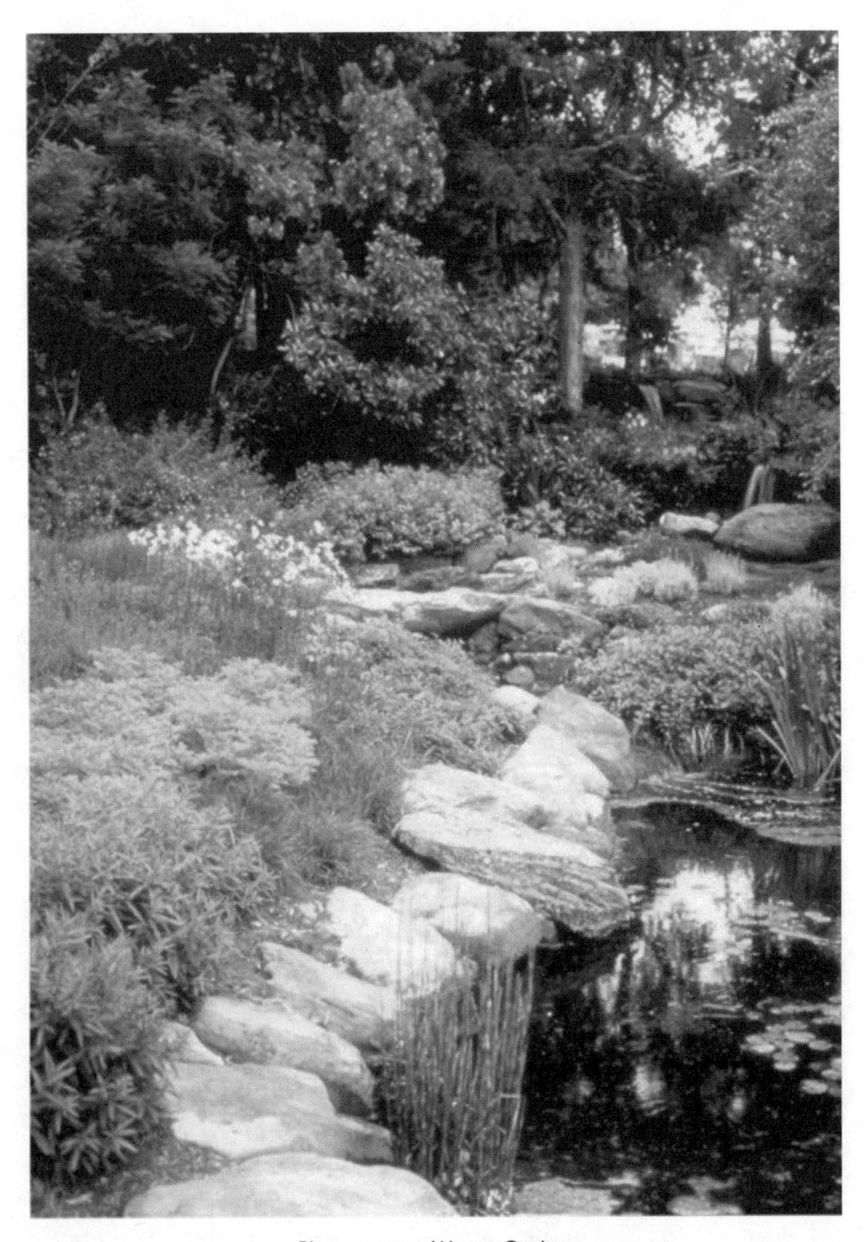

Photo courtesy Weston Gardens

Driving Instructions: Weston Gardens in Bloom is not difficult to find, but you will wonder, once you leave the Interstate, how you could have passed from an urban to a rural environment so quickly.

From IH-20 on the south side of Fort Worth, exit at Anglin Drive (Exit 441) and go south for 2.3 miles. The nursery will be on your left, and that's where you will probably want to park. You can then walk across the road to the demonstration gardens.

McKinney

Crump's Gardens Christmas Open House

3163 Farm Road 543
McKinney, Texas 75071
972-562-0700; 972-542-3346

Fee: Free.

Accessibility: Excellent in retail, poor in greenhouses.

Days and Hours: Weekend after Thanksgiving, with Open House on Sunday afternoon, from 12-5. The store is open year round, but the greenhouses may be toured only during this event.

Garden Type: Greenhouses full of poinsettias.

Garden Size: Five spectacular acres under glass, showing off 70,000 poinsettias in bloom.

Themes and Special Features: Continuous greenhouse tours during open house. This is a popular holiday event in this part of the state, as folks come to revel in the color and choose the florals and greenery that will brighten their homes for the upcoming holidays. Besides all the thousands of poinsettias in glorious shades of red, pink, white, and yellow to choose from, they find high-quality hanging baskets, green and blooming houseplants, and holiday wreathes, either made or grown right here on this family-owned property.

Bird Alert: Since it's November, you should spot more than one red-tailed hawk in the vicinity. Check out bare branches among the taller trees. American kestrel is also a good possibility on the road out to the greenhouses. Northern mockingbirds are almost always around.

Tour Policy: Tours are self-guided.

Driving Instructions: From U.S. Highway 75 north of McKinney, take Exit 43 onto Farm Road 543 west. Watch for the greenhouses on your left within about a mile.

The Heard Natural Science Museum & Wildlife Sanctuary Native Plant Garden

One Nature Place
McKinney, Texas 75069
972-562-5566
email: info@heardmuseum.org
http://www.heardmuseum.org

Fee: Entrance to the garden is free; admission to the museum and nature trail is $5 for adults and $3 for children from 3 to 12 and for seniors 60+.

Accessibility: Excellent.

Days and Hours: Open 9-5 Monday through Saturday, 1-5 Sunday. Closed on major holidays.

Garden Type: Glorious in spring and fall, this Texas Native Plant Display Garden harbors over 200 plant species, including some seldom seen in public collections, like Texas aloe and the native black cherry.

Photo courtesy The Heard Museum

It's especially strong in trees, shrubs, and subshrubs that might be adaptable to urban landscapes.

Garden Size: About half an acre in the garden; 289 acres in the wildlife sanctuary.

Themes and Special Features: One of the most compelling features of the garden is a constructed dry-stream bed of river rocks and small boulders. One corner of it hides a small waterfall and pond, lined with water clover, a very natural-looking vignette reminiscent of the Hill Country.

The Gardens: The plants you'll find thriving here tend to be the tough ones. The effect is of a natural setting, planned and planted, but left to survive largely on its own. Different species come into flower at different times, and when heat and drought bear down, the beds can show some stress, but then, so does any planting that's not babied through the hard times. The point is, they survive, and for many homeowners, seeing which natives will do that and look decent most of the time, too, is a real learning experience. Visitors especially appreciate the signage identifying plant species throughout the area.

Don't-Miss Feature: Look for frogs in or near the pond.

Bird Alert: This sanctuary is well known for the wide variety of birds that make their homes here, with over 270 species having been recorded. Eastern bluebirds will be here year round. You may see a greater roadrunner hunting along the rural roads nearby, and hear Bewick's wren calling from the woods. Both red-tailed hawks and northern harriers may sail overhead.

The Heard Raptor Center, also located on the grounds, is a rehabilitation center for injured raptors, like hawks and eagles. It is not open to the public, but a Birds of Prey Festival is held in the fall, with live birds and guided walks on nature trails. For details, call 976-562-5566.

Sponsored Activities and Tours: Call for information about horticultural programs or guided tours along the five-mile nature trail. You may ask, too, about renting facilities for a wedding in the woods, corporate picnics, anniversaries, and other special occasions. In April each year, the largest Native Plant Sale in Texas takes place here. Members of the Museum get first shot at over 300 varieties of native Texas trees, shrubs, grasses, and flowers, a good reason to join. Memberships are available on several levels.

Volunteer and Support Opportunities: Volunteers have always been a vital part of this organization, helping out in all areas, from the garden to the museum to the wildlife sanctuary. Give them a call, they'll be happy to hear from you.

Gift Shop: One of the best nature stores in the Metroplex area, this shop presents an excellent selection of plant and wildlife-related books, toys, and gifts.

Driving Instructions: From U.S. Highway 75, take Exit 38A and follow the signs to the Heard Museum. Or, from State Highway 5, turn east onto Farm Road 1378, about three miles south of McKinney in the little township of Fairview. The museum is on the left, about a mile down this road. Watch for the sign.

The World Collection of Crape Myrtles

Crape Myrtle Trails of McKinney
Foundation
P.O. Box 2909
McKinney, Texas 75069
972-516-4235
email: info@crapemyrtletrails.com

 **Fee:** Free.

Accessibility: Varies; much of the collection can be viewed from an automobile.

 **Days and Hours:** From mid to late summer, anytime there's enough light to see color.

Garden Type: Plantings in public areas along city thoroughfares and in city parks.

Garden Size: Twenty miles when complete.

Themes and Special Features: This ambitious project, begun in 1999, is in the process of planting thousands of crape myrtles around the city, including specimens of every known cultivar in existence. With the cooperation of local garden clubs, area businesses, the city of McKinney, Texas A&M University, and gardening radio personality and author Neil Sperry, the Foundation intends to create a unique and world-class planting here that will attract the attention of visitors from everywhere.

The Gardens: Crape myrtles love Texas and Texans love them. At just the time each year when it seems that every blooming thing has shut down for a summer siesta, crape myrtles start bursting into bloom, and they are not shy about it, either. They lift arms full of soft, brilliant luxurious blossoms up to the sun and shake them in the hot wind and laugh as the temperature edges over a hundred. Except for lantanas and a few other really tough natives, nothing else braves the summer as beautifully as crape myrtle. White, pink, lavender, maroon, red as a watermelon, and purple as a grape—crape myrtles don't quit. Different varieties bloom at different times, allowing for a carefully planned succession of bloom covering the summer months.

You can see such a plan in action along a mile of U.S. Highway 380, just west of U.S. Highway 75. Another stretch lies along Eldorado Parkway, between Texas Highway 5 and Orchid Drive, about a five-mile drive. Look for more plantings over the next few years.

Tour Policy: Tours are self-guided driving tours.

Volunteer and Support Opportunities: This nonprofit organization makes strategic partnerships with civic and corporate interests, but individual memberships play a huge part in accomplishing the goal of making McKinney a destination city. Friends of the Trail memberships are available. Use the contact information above.

Driving Instructions: McKinney is located north of Dallas on U.S. Highway 75 or Texas Highway 5.

Paris

Pine Branch Daylily Garden

Bobby and Aileen Castlebury, Owners
Route 1, Box 93
Brookston, Texas 75421
903-785-0206
email: casdaylily@paristexas.net

This is a private residence. Call to arrange a time to view the gardens. June and July are the most productive months.

Fee: Free.

Accessibility: Varies. Call for details, especially after rains.

Days and Hours: Open daily during spring and early summer. Call for specific hours.

Garden Type: This is a working daylily farm, with expansive display beds, including an American Hemerocallis Society display and one thousand registered varieties of daylilies; also includes thousands of seedlings each year from the owner's own hybridizing.

Photo courtesy Pine Branch Daylily Garden

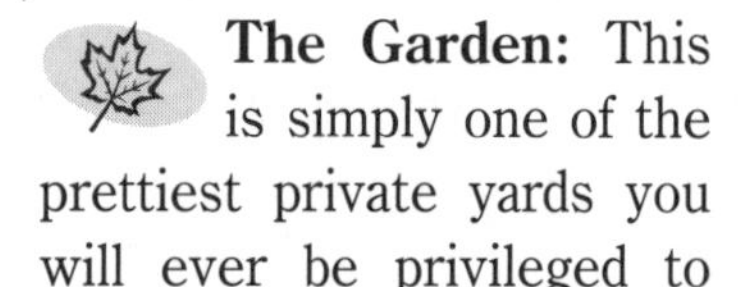

The Garden: This is simply one of the prettiest private yards you will ever be privileged to visit. Great swaths of green lawn, neat colorful beds of lilies of infinite variety, clear, deep ponds where great blue herons hunt, and tall, cool pine trees backing it all up, makes for a park-like setting. Meander around the grounds, and enjoy the blooms, making notes about the lilies you want to own. Seedlings of most varieties are available for purchase.

Themes and Special Features: The owners delight in the birdlife that teems in the pines and around the ponds, and so will you. Purple martins nest here.

Bird Alert: Eastern bluebird, tufted titmouse, and ruby-throated hummingbird are at home here. Red-bellied woodpeckers haunt the woods.

Sponsored Activities: The Castleburys participate in the American Hemerocallis Society Display Garden Tour during peak bloom period, which means late May and early June in this area.

Tour Policy: Tours are self-guided with lots of good signs helping you identify cultivars and decide which ones you want to buy.

Driving Instructions: From U.S. Highway 82 about a mile and a half west of Paris, turn north onto Farm Road 1510 and go about ½ mile. You will see the farm on the right, where the daylilies are blooming.

Sherman

Texoma Landscapes

5020 Texoma Parkway
(U.S. Highway 91 North)
Sherman, Texas 75090
903-465-5456
email: jcastro@texoma.net
http://texomalandscapes.com

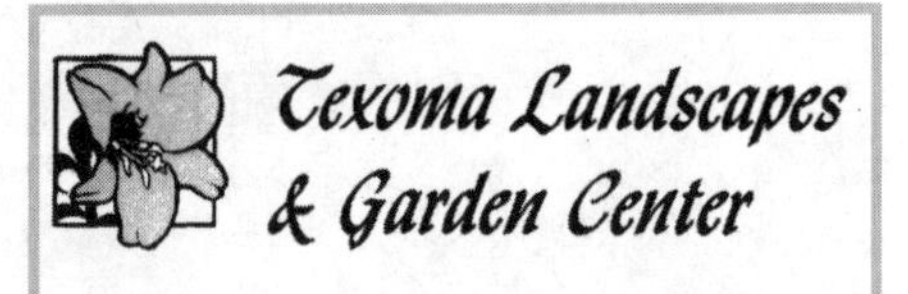

Fee: Free.

Accessibility: Good. Someone here will be able to lend a hand, if needed.

Days and Hours: Open Monday through Saturday, 9-5.

Garden Type: Display garden for a retail nursery and landscape company.

Garden Size: Backyard sized.

Organic Maintenance: Planted and maintained entirely without synthetic fertilizers or chemicals.

Themes and Special Features: Native and adapted perennials and annuals for four-season color. Two nifty water gardens.

The Garden: This engaging little garden was built to showcase the landscape and water-garden design talents of owner Jonathan Castro. All organic and lushly planted, it features two lovely backyard-sized water features, complete with falls, koi, and lilies. A rough-cedar arbor provides shade, and several benches invite visitors to sit and enjoy the flowers, butterflies, and birds.

Don't overlook the flowerbeds located near the entrance, which contain some of the showiest plants. Since they are kept groomed as a display for potential customers, all the beds are attractive from March until mid-November, with strong successional bloom throughout the growing season. If you're looking for inspiration for landscaping your own North Texas property, you'll find lots of practical ideas here.

Don't-Miss Feature: Walk around to the back of the westernmost waterfall and see the stacked-rock wall, with different varieties of sedum cascading out of it. There's also a mammoth peppermint bed here that, the last time I saw it, was about 25 feet by 12, and spreading.

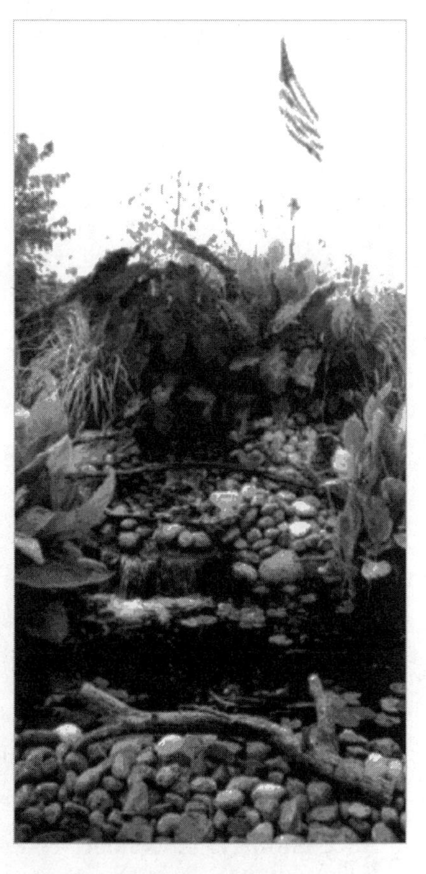

Bird Alert: Mockingbirds will greet you here, any time of the year you visit.

Sponsored Activities: This nursery sponsors a spring tour of water gardens at private homes. Contact the number above in early spring for each year's details.

Tour Policy: You're welcome to bring as many folks as you like to stroll through the property, though if you have more than a vanload you will have to take the tour in stages. Owner Jonathon Castro will be glad to tell your group about his garden if you call ahead to let him know you're coming.

Gift Shop: This is a full-service retail nursery, so take the time to visit the greenhouses, where you will find an exceptional selection of perennials, natives, and old roses at competitive prices. You won't find much in the way of gifts here, but sometimes some interesting outdoor sculpture turns up.

Driving Instructions: From U.S. Highway 75 just north of Sherman, take the exit for Farm Road 691 and turn east. Drive until the road ends at a traffic light. Turn right and get into the left lane, so you can make the first U-turn. Once you make it, immediately look to your right for a big flowerbed and driveway. This place can be hard to spot on the first go-round, because it's in such an unlikely location, tucked into a narrow spot between two manufactured-housing show lots, but if you miss it the first time, it's simple enough to go around again.

Waco

The Earle-Harrison House and Gardens on Fifth Street

The Earle-Harrison House
& Gardens on 5th Street

1901 N. 5th Street
Waco, Texas 76708
254-753-2032
email: samlehh@clearsource.net
http://www.earleharrison.com

Fee: The gardens are free but do not include tours of the house. Pick up a self-tour guide on the front porch of the mansion.

Accessibility: Excellent. Follow the instructions in Driving Directions below.

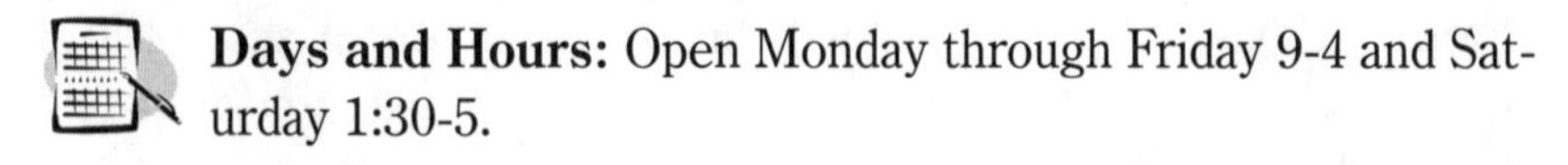

Days and Hours: Open Monday through Friday 9-4 and Saturday 1:30-5.

Garden Type: Private estate garden maintained by the G.H. Pape Foundation, Friends of the Gardens, and other volunteers.

Garden Size: Five acres.

Themes and Special Features: This visitor-friendly garden offers leisurely strolls along neat pink brick paths through perennial beds featuring old roses, daylilies, American beauty berry, and other natives, as well as eye-catching clumps of colorful grasses. Shade gardens of fern and hosta shelter beneath huge live oak trees. An unusual double gazebo may be the first feature to catch your attention.

The Garden: As you explore these magnificent estate grounds, you may think you've been transported to the Deep South. Pecans, magnolias, oaks, crape myrtles, and evergreens of inestimable age shadow a gently rolling parkland. Grassy swaths are punctuated by planting beds and garden features. The Earle-Harrison House dominates the grounds with its Greek-Revival columns and pre-Civil War air, but not to be outdone, the garden boasts a 75-foot-long rose arbor on the opposite side of the grounds. A water garden showcases lilies and other plants, and plans are underway to develop a half-acre children's garden.

You will find garden benches and other seating areas here and there, serving as both an integral part of the overall design and a convenience to the visitor.

The overall impression of this place is one of quiet and dignified beauty, suitable for meditation. On a recent October visit, I found myself alone except for a horde of monarch butterflies making the most of the late-blooming lantana. Its charm shines in the winter, too, with the warm old buildings and towering live oaks anchoring the estate firmly to Texas soil.

Don't-Miss Features: A planting of yellow rise 'n' shine roses near the house is breathtaking in bloom in spring and early summer.

Bird Alert: Carolina wrens may fuss at you here, emitting much too much sheer volume of song per ounce of bird. Woodpeckers often set up a racket, too, both the red-bellied and the downy. In the summer you may glimpse black-chinned hummingbirds and both eastern and western kingbirds. In winter look for northern flicker, yellow-bellied sapsucker, and dark-eyed junco.

Sponsored Activities: The Junior Master Gardener Program administered by the Texas Agricultural Extension Service has a strong presence here. A garden show and sales event held on the grounds in

April brings speakers and other garden experts into the community and sponsors a delightful array of children's activities.

Tour Policy: Garden tours are self-guided, with a map available on the porch of the Earle-Harrison House. Private tours of the house can be arranged by calling the number above. The first floor is accessible.

Volunteer and Support Opportunities: Memberships and sponsorships for specific projects are available on several levels. Volunteers are always needed. Call the number above to get involved or make a donation.

Driving Instructions: From IH-35 or downtown, take 4th Street west. You can follow the signs directing you to Cameron Zoo. As you pass the zoo on your right, don't get too distracted by the pretty plantings at the entrance gate, because you need to be prepared to turn left right away onto Ellis Street. Then, at the end of the block, turn left again onto 5th Street going east. You will turn left again almost immediately into the semicircular driveway of the Earle-Harrison House. If a space is available, you may park here. If not, go ahead back to 5th Street and watch for a small blue sign on the left marking the driveway to the Pape Garden Center. If you turn in here, you will find a spacious parking lot in the back, with direct access to the garden.

Homestead Heritage Traditional Crafts Village

P.O. Box 869
Elm Mott, Texas 76640
254-829-2981
http://www.homesteadheritage.com

 **Fee:** Small fee

Accessibility: Varies considerably. Call for information.

Days and Hours: The Village is open Monday through Saturday 10 to 6.

Garden Type: A working farm featuring a herb garden, perennial borders, old roses, and vegetable gardens.

Garden Size: Plantings are scattered around the grounds. The herb garden is larger than most such.

Organic Maintenance: This is an all-organic establishment.

Themes and Special Features: Tour a small village built by a Christian group to preserve and exhibit homesteading skills and crafts, including pottery making, wood crafting, spinning and weaving, and more. The gardens are an important part of this operation.

The Gardens: A working herb garden hides just beyond the blacksmith shop. Here, you will find colorful and useful herbs laid out in dedicated beds. The farm, which can be toured via a hayride on Saturdays, produces the food staples that pioneers would have relied on in this region 150 years ago. Corn, sorghum, sweet potatoes, melons, black-eyed peas, okra, and tomatoes are the summer crops, with lettuce, chard, collards, and broccoli filling the gardens in winter.

Don't-Miss Feature: Take a look at the healthy roses that are being grown here without chemical sprays. Wonder how they do it? It's all in the variety selection. As beautiful as they are, the roses here are among the toughest old roses available. Disease free and almost always in bloom, Caldwell pink forms a backdrop upon which to view the cool, exotic bloom of passionflower vine. Around the Deli, dark red Martha Gonzalez sets a no-nonsense tone for the flowerbeds.

Bird Alert: Mourning dove, yellow-billed cuckoo, and downy woodpeckers nest in the area. Overhead, you may spy Mississippi kite and red-tailed hawk.

Sponsored Activities: Seminars, fairs, and festivals keep the grounds bustling almost year round. The annual Craft and Children's

Fair held over Thanksgiving weekend features craft and skills demonstrations; classes usually focus on organic growing techniques. Special events are scheduled for Memorial Day and Labor Day, too.

Tour Policy: Pick up a map at the visitor center for a self-guided tour of the village, including the herb garden. Conducted tours of the farm take place on Saturdays and during special events. You can schedule a special group tour by calling 254-829-0417.

Gift Shop: The barn, housed in a restored 200-year-old building, showcases the arts and crafts made in the village, including herbal vinegars, soaps, and wreaths, quilts, pottery, and furniture. Across the parking lot, Homestead Farms Deli serves sandwiches and homemade desserts.

Driving Instructions: From IH-35, take Exit 343 and turn west on Farm Road 308. Three miles down the road, turn north onto Farm Road 933 and then west (left) onto Halbert Lane. If you're watching, you'll see a small sign. The farm lies about half a mile down this country lane.

Weatherford

Chandor Gardens

Chandor Gardens

710 W. Simmons
Weatherford, Texas 76086
817-613-1700
email: chamur@aol.com
http://www.chandorgardens.com

Fee: Adults $6; Children 12 and under $4.

Accessibility: Good to somewhat limited. Call for details.

Days and Hours: Open Saturday 9-4 and Sunday 1-4, mid-April through mid-November; may be closed in August.

Garden Type: Private estate garden built in the 1930s by British artist Douglas Chandor on the grounds of his wife's family mansion, which is now the private residence of owners Chuck and Melody Bradford. The house is not included in the garden tour.

Garden Size: Four acres; a helpful map is available at the entry.

Themes and Special Features: A Chinese theme carries through with oriental artifacts, but is rendered largely with native plants and stones. Elements of English, European, and cottage gardens are integrated into the setting, as well. There are especially well-executed shade gardens, a forty-foot man-made waterfall, featuring stones weighing up to 15 tons, and an English bowling green.

The Garden: Often extolled for the charm of its Chinese elements, this garden is one to be experienced slowly and savored—for its history, its romance, and its seamless marrying of the

Photo courtesy Chandor Gardens

native and the exotic. To hurry through it would be to risk missing its core, the ancient trees and the stones—the very heart of Texas and the heart of this garden.

These are the rocks I grew up with, red and brown and rugged. Here they line paths, raise beds, and define plantings. Hoisted into monoliths to flank waterfalls, cemented into ranks to line stream beds, poised as platforms for artwork from another continent, another culture, they define this exquisite garden without dominating it.

The man who first envisioned and then executed this garden was an artist of great achievement. Queen Elizabeth II, Prime Minister Winston Churchill, and President Franklin D. Roosevelt all commissioned portraits by him, and his paintings are still on display in the Texas State Capitol building, as well as in the National Portrait Gallery in Washington, D.C. Working from 1936 until his death in 1953, he fashioned many of the garden's features with his own hands, and it still bears his distinctive stamp.

Chandor Gardens drew thousands of visitors from the 1950s into the 1970s, but with the deaths of the original owners, deteriorated until 1994, when Melody and Chuck Bradford of Aledo bought it and began restoring the property. They did so with deep respect for the original, and today it endures as an outstanding example of how native plants can be integrated into even the most exotic landscape to wonderful effect.

Don't-Miss Feature: Look to your left at the end of the long allee-type entrance for a path to the Dragon Fountain, and near the mansion for the magnificent curving pergola planted with climbing roses, Cecile Brunner, and lavender lassie.

Bird Alert: Black-chinned hummingbird, northern mockingbird, northern cardinal, blue jay, Carolina chickadee, Bewick's wren, rufous-sided towhee, and a variety of sparrows may be found here. Woodpeckers abound. Eastern bluebirds and painted buntings may be spotted occasionally.

Tour Policy: You will need reservations for a group tour. Call the number above for details.

Driving Instructions: From IH-20, take Exit 408 and go north into town. Turn west (left) on W. Simmons Street and continue to the end of the road. Parking can be somewhat haphazard, but you should be able to find a spot on the street.

Whitewright

Whitewright Old Rose and Garden Tour

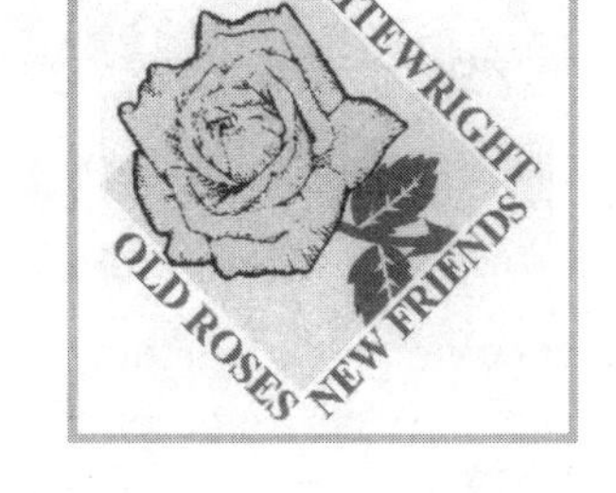

Keep Whitewright Beautiful
125 Grand Street
Whitewright, Texas 75491
903-364-2000
email: bdroberts@texoma.net

Accessibility: Varies from site to site.

Days and Hours: Saturday and Sunday of Mother's Day weekend.

Garden Type: Self-guided tour of about two dozen private home gardens.

The Gardens: This venerable North Texas village springs into life, showing off its collection of cottage gardens, riotous with heritage roses and perennials. Delightful!

Birds to Watch for: Red-tailed hawks will be soaring overhead, maybe a northern harrier, as well. Bewick's wren, Carolina chickadee, Carolina wren, eastern bluebird, northern

Photo courtesy Keep Whitewright Beautiful

mockingbird, northern cardinal, and orchard oriole will be nesting near gardens, and purple martins will be chasing insects through the air. The hummingbirds you spot are ruby-throated.

Driving Instructions: Whitewright lies just off U.S. Highway 69 between Denison and Greenville. Turn east from Hwy. 69 at the sign that points the way to downtown, and follow the street, which curves back to the north, to the center of town.

Extra Treats: While you are in Whitewright, treat yourself to a tour of the delightful **Whitewright Nature and Historical Park** on the east side of town. Lilliputian, like the rest of the town, it contains enough beauty for two or three less-lovingly maintained plantings.

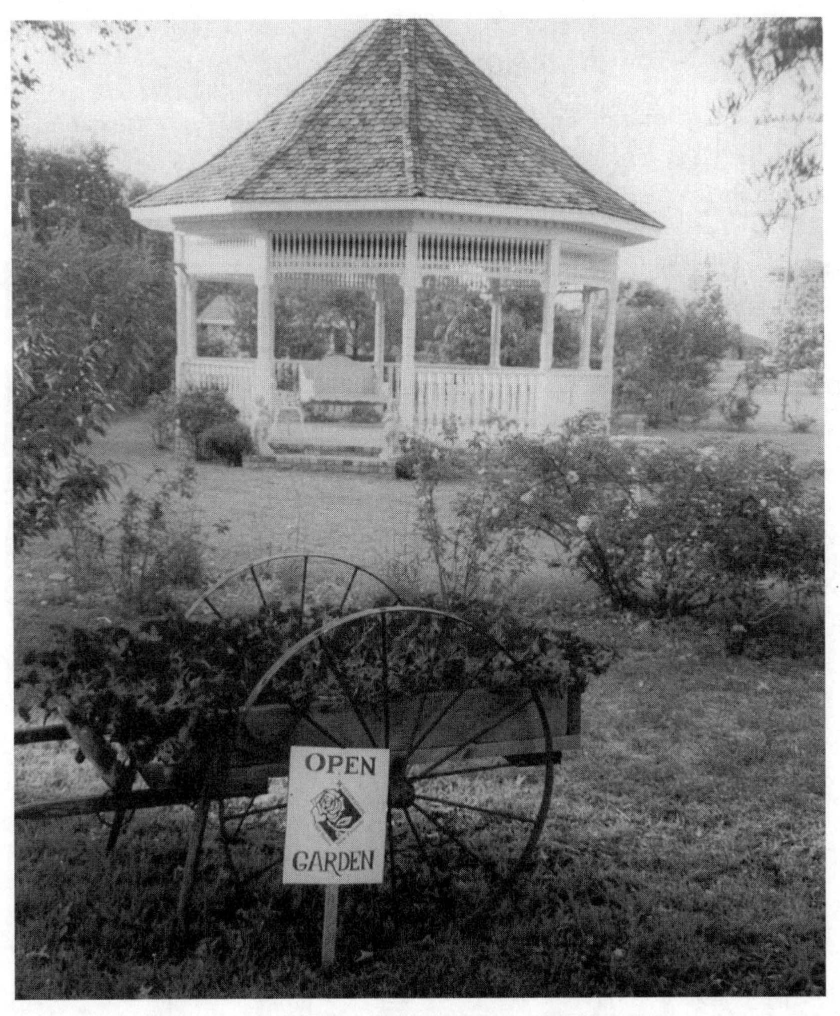

Photo courtesy Keep Whitewright Beautiful

Bird Song in the Garden

I once spent a miserably restless night in the state of Alabama, madc so by a mockingbird singing proudly outside my window all night. It wasn't the noise he made that disturbed me. It was the fact that he was singing songs I didn't know. He was, naturally enough, imitating the ditties of local birds, whose songs I, just as naturally, had never heard. Every time I'd start to drift off, he'd tune up a new one, and my eyes would pop open at the strangeness.

You might say he didn't have a Texas accent. The fact is, birds often sound different from one part of the country to another. Northern cardinals, for instance, have distinct eastern and western "accents." So if the bird song you hear in a Texas garden seems like a different dialect from what you're used to hearing, maybe it is.

Finding More Gardens in North Texas

The **American Hemerocallis** (daylily) **Society** lists three display gardens in the Dallas area, which will be open to the public on specified dates late each spring and often by appointment at other times. Call for information.

Amerson Daylily Garden, Binion Amerson, 972-241-1726

Hillcrest Iris and Daylily Gardens, Hooker and Bonnie Nichols, 214-352-2191

Hurst Park Daylily Garden, Mabel Matthews, 817-268-5189

The **North Texas Water Garden Society** sponsors a quite extensive tour of water gardens at private homes, usually in June. This tour may be self-guided by purchasing a map, or if demand is high enough, a tour bus will be available. For details, contact the society at 214-358-2995.

Further north, **Texoma Landscapes** in Sherman helps to organize an early-summer tour of local water gardens. You can find out this year's dates by calling 903-892-3908.

And in the southerly regions of the area, the **Waco Pond Society** conducts their tour in the fall. Information is available from local nurseries and pet stores.

Part Three

The Gardens of East Texas

Athens, Beaumont, Chandler, Gladewater, Jefferson, Kilgore, Marshall, Nacogdoches, Orange, Tyler

The forests of East Texas were magical to me as a child. Reared on the western prairie and privileged to visit the forest only rarely, I was awe-stricken by the giant pine trees, the flaming gums, the unfailing greenery, and the enchanted fact of flowers blooming throughout the woods in spring. Dogwood, azalea, wisteria, and magnolia created a wonderland on the acid, humus-rich soils of the Piney Woods then, as they still do today. Along the roads, where sun penetrates, wild phlox carpets the right-of-way in hues as rich as the most magnificent tapestry's, and I have seen stretches of country road where narcissus, escaped from early settler's farm sites, have naturalized in golden swaths of fragrant trumpets.

On the western edge of this area lies a savanna of oaks, elms, and nut trees, while the southern perimeter merges into prairie and then into marshland near the Gulf of Mexico, making the area we call "East Texas" over 33 million acres in extent. Upwards of 55 inches of rain a year drench parts of this region, so creeks, rivers, bayous, lakes, and swamps are common features.

Today public gardens thrive throughout the region, and communities celebrate the changing of the seasons with parades and festivals. Cutting-edge horticulture is practiced in Nacogdoches at Stephen F. Austin University's Mast Arboretum. Formal rose gardens flourish in Tyler and Beaumont, despite the humidity, and the state's only full-fledged Shakespeare Garden grows in Kilgore. And what may be the state's quaintest expression of gardening single-mindedness fills the forest with a golden haze as Mrs. Lee's Daffodil Garden in Gladewater greets each spring.

Birds abound here. Populations change with the season, but there is always something to look for along the roads.

In the north, summer brings scissor-tailed flycatcher and dicksissel, cattle egret, and purple martin. In winter, you will notice eastern meadowlark, American kestrel, and, if you look up, bald eagle and northern harrier. Toward the south, watch for roadrunners and buntings, kingbirds and cuckoos, and everywhere eastern bluebird. Near water expect belted kingfisher, great blue heron, wood duck, and American white pelican.

The Great Texas Coastal Birding Trail, a joint project of Texas Parks and Wildlife and the Texas Department of Transportation, has claimed a huge chunk of this real estate as the Big Thicket Loop. You can pick up a map of the birding areas at the Chamber of Commerce in Beaumont or Orange, or contact the TPW at 888-TXBIRDS and select the option for the Upper Trail.

Athens

East Texas Arboretum and Botanical Society

1601 Patterson Road at Highway 175 West
P.O. Box 2231
Athens, Texas 75751
903-675-5630
email: etabs@tvec.net
http://www.eastexasarboretum.org

Fee: $2 per vehicle.

Accessibility: Good in the garden, more challenging on the trail. Call for details.

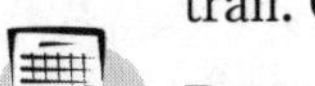

Days and Hours: Daily during daylight hours.

Garden Type: Small but very pretty herb and flower garden backed by nature trail.

Garden Size: The nature trail covers about 100 acres, but only a small part of this area is devoted to cultivation. An 1850s dogtrot house is home to a small museum.

Photo courtesy East Texas Arboretum

The Gardens: Herbs and flowering annuals and perennials decorate a very attractive covered pavilion, and a sparkling water feature will delight the children. But the nature trail is the star here, nature in its wildest state. Started and maintained by a nonprofit organization dedicated to conservation and education, the area focuses on the "arboretum" part of the name. Native trees, shrubs, and wildflowers along a well-marked trail lead the adventurous into a discovery of the beauties of native flora.

Bird Alert: Look for eastern bluebirds nesting in spring.

Sponsored Activities: The Arboretum sponsors workshops and plant sales throughout the year, with topics ranging from butterfly gardening to floral arranging and beyond. A small fee is charged.

Tour Policy: Tours can be arranged by calling the number above.

Volunteer and Support Opportunities: Opportunities abound with this young organization. They'll find something useful for you to do, from clerical duties to guiding tours. No special qualifications are required. Just pitch in.

Memberships are available from the $25 Individual to the $1,000 Friend level, and many of the garden's features are memorials or donations provided by individuals, groups, and businesses in the community.

Driving Instructions: From U.S. Highway 175 west of Athens, turn west (left, if you're coming from town) on Patterson Road just southwest of Loop 317. Watch for the small green Arboretum sign that marks the turn.

The Old Oak Tree

In the town of Athens sits the oldest continuously operating courthouse in the state. One block to the east of the square, you will find a giant red oak tree that was ancient when the courthouse was built in 1850.

Beaumont

Beaumont Botanical Gardens

Beaumont Council of Garden Clubs
6088 Babe Zaharias Drive
Beaumont, Texas 77725
409-842-3135
Beaumont Convention and Visitors Bureau: 800-392-4401
http://www.beaumontbotanicalgardens.com

Fee: Free.

Accessibility: Very friendly to wheelchairs and strollers, and there are shady benches just where the weary need them.

Days and Hours: Daily during daylight hours.

Garden Type: Botanical garden (see also Warren Loose Conservatory).

Garden Size: Twenty-three acres, with lots of winding paths.

Themes and Special Features: Special collections featuring antique and modern roses, double daylilies, bromeliads, herbs, palms, agaves, camellias, and azaleas. Japanese garden, green and white garden, and fragrance garden.

The Gardens: They might almost have called this "The Secret Garden." It's hidden in a city park in an area of town without other tourist attractions, and once you hunt it down and enter its winding paths beneath towering trees, you find yourself on a journey of discovery. Around each corner lies another secret nook, full of interesting or colorful plants and collections.

Check out the pretty patio garden beside the conservatory with its modern water feature and then wander down to the rose garden, and immerse yourself in the Old South full of rose arbors, camellias, hibiscus, and herbs, with Spanish moss waving gently from massive branches above your head.

You will find a small fragrance garden, raised to just the right height, encircling a rustic figure of Saint Fiacre, patron saint of gardeners, a Japanese garden complete with arched wooden bridges and stone lanterns, and a formal rose garden at the very back.

This is a soft garden, all curving paths and hidden nooks, but very accessible throughout. It has been certified by Texas Parks and Wildlife as a Texas Wildscape Demonstration Site and is rich in birds, reptiles, and other critters.

Don't-Miss Feature: The opportunity to feed the mallard and Muscovy ducks and the Embden and Toulouse geese at the pond near the rear of the garden. Take some bread crusts with you.

(Few objects in nature are more beguiling to a toddler than the rear end of a duck in motion. You may want to be prepared to explain that ducks, unlike dogs, do not enjoy being chased.)

Bird Alert: This park, part of the Texas Coastal Birding Trail, is a birder's paradise, with not only large trees to allure songbirds, but nearby wetlands to attract birds of the marsh and shore. Look for Carolina wren, pine warbler, eastern bluebird, Parula warbler, and ruby-throated hummingbird, as well as various hawks, cattle egrets, and Louisiana herons. Woodpeckers include downy, pileated, and red-bellied. Fish crow is a good possibility.

Sponsored Activities: The Beaumont Council of Garden Clubs, which maintains the grounds, holds or sponsors plant sales, lectures, and other public events. They also host a tour of gardens at private homes during the first weekend of May each year. Call the number above for information.

Tour and Rental Policy: Group and school tours are easy to arrange for a $20 fee (plus regular admission for each member of the group). Combine the garden tour with a tour of the Warren Loose Conservatory for only $10 more. They ask that you make arrangements a couple of weeks in advance.

Volunteer and Support Opportunities: You don't need any special qualifications to get your hands in the dirt here. Or, they can use your talents for tour guiding or fund raising, event planning, or go-fering. They'll welcome your call.

Driving Instructions: From IH-10, take Exit 848, Walden Road south (it will look like east). When you come to the traffic light, look straight ahead. The road into the park is small and easy to overlook. What you want to do is go through the light onto Tyrrell Park Road, which leads through the park entrance to the botanic garden on your left.

The Warren Loose Conservatory

Bert & Jack Binks Horticultural Center
Beaumont Council of Garden Clubs
6088 Babe Zaharias Drive
Beaumont, Texas 77725
409-842-3145
Beaumont Convention and Visitors Bureau: 800-392-401

Fee: Adults $3; Seniors $2; Children 6-12 $1

Accessibility: Excellent.

Days and Hours: Open Wednesday through Friday 10-2; Saturday 10-5; Sunday 1-5. (Also open by appointment.)

Garden Type: Glass conservatory displaying thousands of tropical plants.

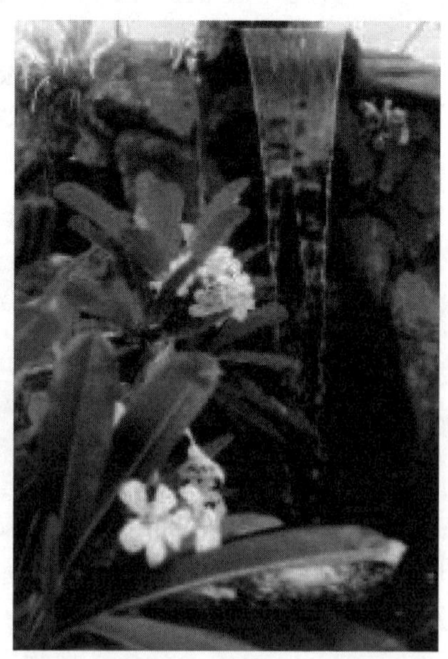

Photo courtesy Beaumont Botanical Garden

Garden Size: At 10,000 square feet, this is a respectable-sized facility.

Themes and Special Features: Here is where the tropics come alive, with a water lily pool full of fantail goldfish, edged by Victorian water lilies from the Amazon, plus foliage and flowering tropical plants of every imaginable description.

The Gardens: Entering through the Binks Horticultural Center, take a moment to look around. You'll find a fountain here, stained glass panels, and an art museum, before you even enter the conservatory. Inside, look for tropical plants, palms, ferns, lilies, and orchids.

Don't-Miss Feature: The animated dinosaur at one end of the conservatory.

Tour and Rental Policy: Tours for groups of 15 or more can be arranged for a $20 fee (plus regular admission for each member of the group). Include the outside garden in your tour for only an additional $10.

Volunteer and Support Opportunities: To get involved, call or write to the address above.

Driving Instructions: From IH-10 on the south side of Beaumont, take Walden Road south; it becomes Tyrrell Park Road, which leads through the park entrance to the Conservatory on your left.

McFaddin-Ward House

1906 McFaddin Avenue
Beaumont, Texas 77701
409-832-2134
info@mcfaddin-ward.org
http://www.mcfaddin-ward.org

THE McFADDIN - WARD HOUSE
Beaumont, Texas

Fee: Small admission fee, depending on how many buildings you plan to visit.

Accessibility: Varies between houses and grounds. Limited.

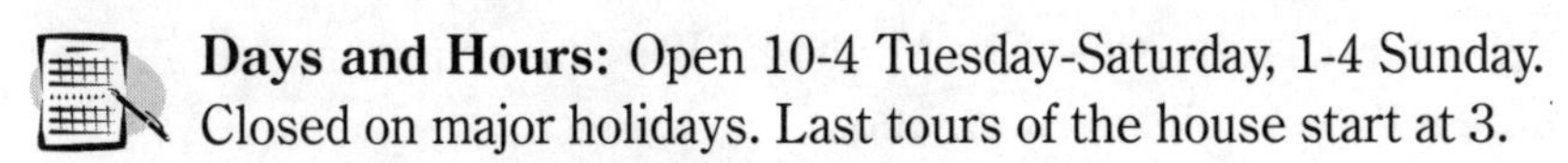

Days and Hours: Open 10-4 Tuesday-Saturday, 1-4 Sunday. Closed on major holidays. Last tours of the house start at 3.

Garden Type: Estate garden on the grounds of a 1906 Beaux Arts Colonial style house.

Garden Size: Three landscaped blocks including buildings; 40,000 square feet in lawns and 20,000 square feet in garden beds.

Photo courtesy McFaddin-Ward House, Beaumont, Texas

The Gardens: Most of the activities here are geared toward preservation and exhibition of the grand old house itself, but for a gardenophile, the grounds are worth meandering around. This is East Texas, so you can expect azaleas, redbuds, dogwoods, tulip magnolia, and wisteria in the early spring and other colorful perennials and annuals throughout the warmer months. A rose garden offers up its bounty almost year round.

Bird Alert: Ruby-throated hummingbird is a summer resident here.

Sponsored Activities: The McFaddin-Ward Museum maintains a volunteer corps. Call for information.

Tour Policy: Tours focus on the house. Reservations are recommended; no children under eight in the house, please.

Driving Instructions: The Visitor Center is in the 1900 block of Calder Street, between North 3rd and North 4th Streets. Take the Calder exit from IH-10 and go east. The Visitor Center will be on your left.

Chandler

Blue Moon Gardens

13062 Farm Road 279
Chandler, Texas 75758
903-852-3897
http://www.bluemoongardens.com

Fee: Free.

Accessibility: Good in most parts of the grounds.

Days and Hours: Open 9-5:30 Monday through Saturday, 12-5 Sunday.

Garden Type: Cottage garden and greenhouses at retail nursery.

Garden Size: Six acres, including retail space.

Organic Maintenance: Encourages use of organic techniques.

Themes and Special Features: Clustered about a farmhouse that's nearly a century old and newer buildings that carry out the same style, this is cottage garden par excellence.

The Gardens: Herbs, perennials, and old-fashioned annuals lend a constantly festive air to this property, secreted among the East Texas pines, far from city lights and other signs of modernity. Cleverly designed display gardens lift the country style to sophisticated heights of expression.

Don't-Miss Feature: Peek at the charming Children's Garden behind the picket fence.

Bird Alert: The rural setting is perfect for birding, yielding purple martins in the spring, indigo and painted buntings in

Photo courtesy Blue Moon Gardens

summer, and American goldfinch and various sparrow species in the winter.

Sponsored Activities: Full-day special events are held here for spring, fall, and Christmas, with speakers, demonstrations, and refreshments. Workshops are held throughout the year in a spacious classroom. Topics are seasonal, ranging from making soaps, wreaths, and other herbal products to growing vegetables successfully.

A garden club, comprised of dedicated gardeners of all levels of expertise, meets once a month for programs and fellowship. Membership in the club brings discounts on store purchases and participation in such club activities as tours of members' private gardens.

Tour Policy: Please call ahead to arrange a group tour.

Gift Shop: Genuine country charm, not the fussified kind, strikes the keynote here. You'll find everything you need to take care of your backyard birds, including nesting boxes, feeders, and baths, as well as whimsical garden art and gifts and herbal products of every conceivable kind.

Driving Instructions: From State Highway 64 a few miles west of Tyler, turn southwest on Farm Road 279 and drive about six miles. Look for the pretty farmhouse gardens on your left.

Gladewater

Mrs. Helen Lee's Daffodil Garden

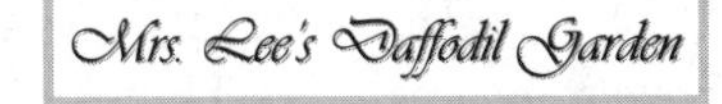

21600 CR 3103
Gladewater, Texas 75647
903-845-5780
http://www.daffodilgarden.com
Also Gladewater Chamber of Commerce: 903-845-5501

Fee: Free.

Accessibility: The garden is highly visible from your vehicle on the four-mile road that wends throughout.

Days and Hours: Open from 10:00-4:30 from mid-February to mid-March. May be closed after heavy rains. Call ahead to determine road conditions and blooming schedules.

Note to Drivers: Vehicles larger than a standard van are not allowed in the garden. Roads are unpaved and bumpy and can be muddy.

Garden Type: Naturalized daffodil meadows on private land.

Garden Size: Twenty acres in bloom on a 700-acre nature preserve. You can make the four-mile drive through the garden in about an hour if you're in a hurry. Plan for longer if you will be taking photographs, birding, or just plain glorying in the spring sunshine.

Themes and Special Features: Some biblical scholars believe that the daffodil, which grows wild throughout the Holy Land, was the "rose" mentioned in the Old Testament.

Here, as in other parts of the state where spring is a real season, during a time of renewal after the cold blasts of January, daffodils are among the first of all the flowers to bloom. Sometimes overeager, they start before winter is truly done, and their dancing yellow heads, many heavy with fragrance, restore life and hope to garden and meadow. As Shakespeare put it, "When daffodils begin to peer...Why, then comes in the sweet o' the year." When daffodils bloom, can spring be far behind?

The Gardens: It's hard to imagine a more unlikely legacy of the Great East Texas Oil Boom of the 1930s than this vast planting of beautifully unpretentious golden daffodils. Widowed in 1954, Mrs. Helen Lee used some of the family fortune to order a literal boxcar load of daffodil bulbs from The Netherlands and planted them, many with her own hands, to naturalize on the gentle slopes and swards of the wilderness under the magnificent pines, oaks, and other native trees and out into the pasture where both cattle and deer still graze today. The result each year, for about five weeks in early spring, is a vista like no other of sparkling, laughing, dancing flowers in a pastoral setting that looks as if it hasn't changed otherwise since this land was first settled.

Two small lakes add to the garden's charm, and a tiny log cabin, built by Mrs. Lee, serves today as a visitor center. Don't fail to stop and sign the guest book here. The number of visitors per year is an important consideration in keeping the place open to the public.

Mrs. Lee's Garden is one of the truly hidden treasures of Texas. So well concealed is it in the depths of the East Texas forest that you'll be tempted to let out a string behind you as you go to make sure you can find your way back through the maze of narrow country roads. But don't worry. Once you know it's there, it's easy enough to find and a breeze to find your way back from (see Driving Instructions below).

Don't-Miss Feature: Wild white-tailed deer grazing throughout the garden.

Birds to Watch for: Eastern bluebirds make their home here, along with brown-headed nuthatch, great blue heron, indigo bunting, red-cockaded woodpecker, plus threatened or endangered species, American peregrine falcon, Arctic peregrine falcon, bald eagle, and loggerhead shrike.

Sponsored Activities: A Wildlife Management Plan, in conjunction with Texas Parks and Wildlife, has been established to protect and promote the wildlife found here in all its diversity.

Tour Policy: All tours are self-guided. No reservations required.

Volunteer and Support Opportunities: To volunteer your services or make a tax-deductible donation, contact the Helen Lee Foundation at the address above.

Driving Instructions: From U.S. 271, turn east on Smith County Road 3104, about 5.5 miles south of Gladewater. After one and a half miles, turn right onto Smith County Road 3103. Go one-fourth mile to the garden entrance.

"Only think, to open in all this wind, and so cold—isn't it beautiful? It's much more beautiful than flowers that come in the summer."

Richard Jeffries, 1887

Jefferson

Jessie Allen Wise Garden Club Historical Pilgrimage Tour

Jefferson Historic Walking Tours
Marion County Chamber of Commerce
118 North Vale Street
Jefferson, Texas 75657
1-888-GO-RELAX
email: thechamber@jefferson-texas.com

Fee: Walking tours are free. The Pilgrimage is $12 for adults and $3 for children 10 and under.

Accessibility: Varies considerably. Call for information.

Days and Hours: You can take the walking tours anytime, although mid-March through May will find the most in bloom. The Historic Pilgrimage takes place the first weekend of May.

Garden Type: The whole village of Jefferson turns into a garden in the spring, making a leisurely drive or stroll around town an adventure in color and fragrance. Stop by the Excelsior House Hotel at 211 W. Austin to pick up a map that will guide you on walking tours through two historic districts.

During the Pilgrimage in May, some private gardens built around beautiful old homes are open to the public for the annual Tour of Homes.

In addition, over 50 bed and breakfast establishments are located here, many of them with landscaped gardens, and while their grounds are not open to the general public, if you are staying in one, inquire about the garden. For some, it's a major attraction.

Photo courtesy Marion County Chamber of Commerce

Gift Shop: Jefferson is absolutely bursting at its tiny little seams with antique and gift shops, as well as places to eat. Plan to spend some time exploring the offerings.

Driving Instructions: State Highway 49 and U.S. Highway 59 intersect in the heart of the East Texas Piney Woods. There lies the town of Jefferson.

Kilgore

Texas Shakespeare Garden

1100 block of Brook Drive, one block east of U.S. Highway 259
Kilgore Improvement and Beautification Association
Kilgore Chamber of Commerce
813 N. Kilgore St.
Kilgore, Texas 75662
903-984-5022
info@ci.kilgore.tx.us

Fee: Free.

Accessibility: Excellent.

Days and Hours: Open daily during daylight hours.

Garden Type: Authentic Shakespeare garden.

Garden Size: About one fifth of an acre.

Themes and Special Features: The idea behind a Shakespeare garden is to plant specimens of some of the many flowers, shrubs, trees, and herbs mentioned in Shakespeare's plays. A great deal of research went into making this representation as authentic as possible. Here you will find the expected herbs: lavender, rosemary, mints and rue, but also the less celebrated narcissus, columbine, carnation, and wild strawberry.

Of especial interest to historians, rosarians, and students of the Bard are the Damask Eglantine roses, a truly antique rose form that we know would have been around in the sixteenth century. This rose boasts a sweet apple fragrance in its foliage, as well as its small pink flowers, and has been known at various times in history by the folk name "sweet briar." It's not the easiest rose to grow in East Texas, since it was bred for cooler, wetter climes, but the gardeners here have backed it up with charming and reliable newer heirloom roses like The Fairy and Louis Phillippe.

The Garden: The garden is a reflection of this community's commitment to Kilgore College and the annual Texas Shakespeare Festival, which since 1986 has enchanted thousands of theater fans with top-notch productions of the Bard's works, as well as more modern plays, musicals, and children's productions. Garden clubs, civic groups, and private citizens have worked together to make the garden possible.

Remarkable as much in its design and layout as in its plantings, this small garden exudes charm in its artful use of classic garden features, brick and stone, concrete and brass. Curved paths radiate from a central pedestal and meander gently to decorative gates or benches. Proportion is exquisite. Plant selections are guided by literary reference but not ruled by them. Native salvias and herbs help extend the color of the beds, while ferns, lilies, and honeysuckle remind us where the heart of this garden lies.

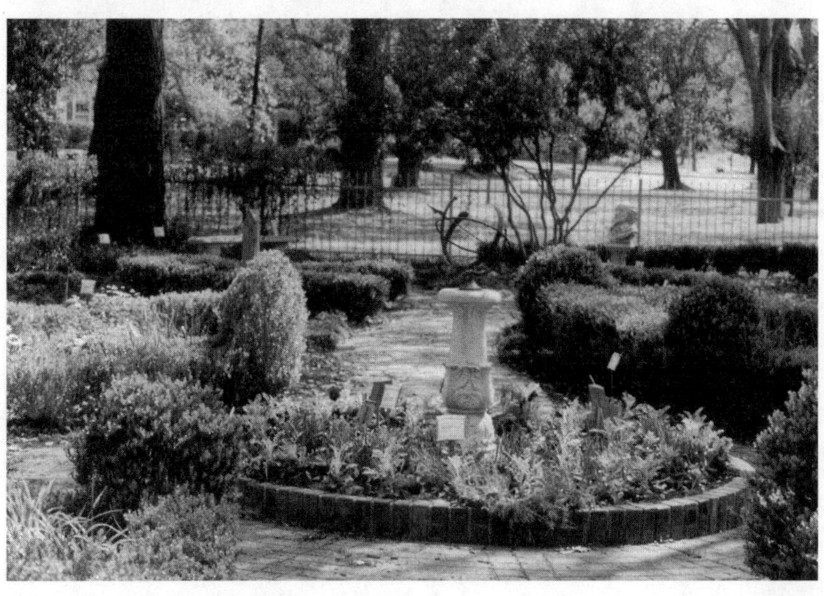

Bird Alert: This wooded area, though urban, is rich with bird life. Gray catbird, Carolina wren, and even painted and indigo buntings are possible.

Tour Policy: Tours are self-guided. Watch for signs identifying plants and quoting appropriate phrases from the works of Shakespeare.

Volunteer and Support Opportunities: Contact Kilgore Improvement and Beautification at P.O. Box 1524, Kilgore, Texas 75663.

Driving Instructions: U.S. Highway 259 runs north and south past the campus of Kilgore College. Watch for Brook Drive turning east between the Fine Arts Center and the Child Development Center on the campus.

Marshall

Starr Family State Historical Park

407 West Travis Street
Marshall, Texas 75670
903-935-3044; 800-792-1112
http://www.tpwd.state.us/park/starrfam

Fee: Free. Fee for museum tours.

Accessibility: Variable; call for more information.

Days and Hours: Grounds open 10-4 Friday and Saturday, 1-5 Sunday, and other times by appointment (call the number above). Closed Thanksgiving, Christmas, and New Year's Days.

Garden Type: Grounds of historical estate.

Garden Size: The park covers just over three acres.

Themes and Special Features: The emphasis here is on history. There are guided and self-guided tours of three historic homes and a schoolhouse, as well as of the gardens.

The Gardens: Come in the spring for the best show. Azaleas, dogwoods, fruit trees, and other early bloomers light up the woods here, as they do all through East Texas. The effect is breathtaking when everything is in full bloom. Later in the year, just enjoy the shade from the towering trees. After Thanksgiving, the houses will be decorated in a Victorian motif for participation in Marshall's famous Wonderland of Lights festival, when almost 10 million lights set the city ablaze.

Bird Alert: Purple martins nest nearby in the summer. Winter sparrows include vesper and LeConte's.

Tour Policy: The gardens are popular for weddings and receptions. Parts of the buildings can also be rented. There is even a bed and breakfast facility in one of the houses, which can sleep up to four people. Reservations are required for that. Tours of the whole grounds can be arranged for groups by calling ahead.

Driving Instructions: From IH-20, exit onto U.S. Highway 59 North. Turn west (left) on Travis Street and continue past South Grove Street.

Nacogdoches

Stephen F. Austin Mast Arboretum

P.O. Box 13000
Nacogdoches, Texas 75962-3000
(located on Wilson Drive on the east side of the Stephen F. Austin State University campus; see Driving Instructions below)
936-468-4343
http://www.sfasu.edu/ag/arboretum

 **Fee:** Free.

Accessibility: Excellent to fair, improving all the time; access is best from the parking lot behind the Agriculture Building into the Shade Garden.

 **Days and Hours:** Open daily during daylight hours.

Garden Type: Arboretum and display gardens for research and education.

Garden Size: Nineteen acres.

Themes and Special Features: Here you will find a large garden built entirely around themes. These include a superb herb garden, mixed borders featuring native and adapted flowering perennials, beds dedicated to daylilies, ferns, bog plants, and camellias, vines, tropicals, and butterfly plants, and a full 16 beds of named azaleas. There is also a Children's Garden.

The Gardens: They call this place a "living laboratory." As the first arboretum to be established at a Texas university, and its 19 acres serve as a classroom, not only for students and faculty, but also for the nursery industry and the public. The Horticulture

Program within the Agriculture Department of the school's College of Education maintains the garden, with the help of a corps of volunteers from all walks of life.

The Herb Garden offers dark pink and red roses blooming against a backdrop of silver artemisia and deep-green rosemaries. Eucalyptus, mullein, scented geraniums, and echinacea vie with lemon-scented herbs to perfume the air. In the Elking Environment, lilies, cannas, hibiscus, and elephant ears crowd the banks. The Daylily Garden boasts "an almost complete collection of the Stout Medal Series," courtesy of the local chapter of the American Hemerocallis Society.

Across the parking lot to the east, a Shade Garden is home to unusual plants like ligularia and illicium, as well as ferns, hostas, azaleas, camellias, lilies, and mallows. There seem to be dozens of different gingers. Is that a cardamom? Wow. If you're overwhelmed, take advantage of one of the many benches that line the path, sit a while, and contemplate the huge old native oaks and pines that make this a true arboretum.

Don't-Miss Feature: See the Carolina jessamin covering five huge arches across the creek southeast of the Agriculture Building if you're here in spring. From late summer to fall, enjoy the ornamental grasses in the borders south of the building. Roses along the parking lot bloom many months in the year, and azalea varieties include both spring and fall bloomers.

On the southeast corner of the Ag Building, you'll find an old-fashioned bottle tree made of cobalt blue bottles, a replica of ornaments that once were staples of southern gardens.

Bird Alert: You can hear red-headed or pileated woodpeckers in the forest. They both nest in this area. Carolina chickadee is here, too, along with tufted titmouse. You might spot any of four different vireos. Many warblers spend the summer in this part of the country, as do eastern wood-pewee and summer tanager.

Sponsored Activities: Galas and festivals with plant sales and tours guided by experts take place in spring and fall. A lecture series for the public meets monthly. For information, call 936-468-1832.

Tour and Rental Policies: Pick up a map/brochure from the main office in the Agriculture Building. You'll be glad you have it as you guide yourself through the garden. Groups of 15 or more can arrange a guided tour with seven days notice by calling 936-468-1832. Call the same number if you're dreaming of a wedding in a wonderful garden setting.

Volunteer and Support Opportunities: The professionals here welcome any help that's offered. No special credentials or degrees needed. There is also a formal Friends organization. To find out how you can help, call 936-468-1832.

Driving Instructions: Loop 224 circles the city of Nacogdoches, so you will approach it no matter which way you come into town. Turn east on the loop. When you reach University Drive, turn north if you came into town from the south; turn south if you came into town from the north. University will take you to the east side of the Stephen F. Austin campus, where you will turn west onto East College Street and then south onto Wilson Drive. The Agriculture Building, which anchors the Arboretum, is the last building on the block on the east side of the street, just before you get to the grassy sports fields. There are parking lots on the west side of the street, as well as behind the Ag Building. If you're going to spend the day here or be a frequent visitor, check with the University Police on College Street for a visitor's permit.

Parking for the Ruby M. Mize Azalea Garden is currently behind the William R. Johnson Coliseum north of the gardens. You can get to the lot from University Drive.

Ruby M. Mize Azalea Garden

Stephen F. Austin State University
P.O. Box 13000
Nacogdoches, Texas 75962-3000
(located on the far east side of the Stephen F. Austin State University campus; see Driving Instructions below)
936-468-4343
http://www.sfasu.edu/ag/arboretum

 **Fee:** Free.

Accessibility: Good. A bit rough at the time of my last visit, but they are working to improve it all the time. Benches, resting spots, and places for contemplation are also an important part of this developing garden.

 **Days and Hours:** Open daily during daylight hours.

Garden Type: Display and test beds for ornamentals adapted to local growing conditions.

Garden Size: Forty beds with more than two miles of trails to wander.

Themes and Special Features: Plant collections include 4,500 azaleas, 200 camellias, and 180 varieties of Japanese maple in the middle of a forest of old loblolly pines.

The Gardens: This colorful garden is a delight to the senses any time of year. Many camellias bloom in winter, some in the fall; Japanese maples light up the landscape nine months of the year; azaleas offer displays throughout the spring, with some blooming again as late as November. Sweetgums light up the forest in the fall, and pecan trees drop their bounty in winter. And those big ole pines are a joy to smell anytime.

What was until the late 1990s eight acres of weedy bottomland is now a premier garden reaching for world class.

Don't-Miss Feature: At the middle of the garden, the Council Ring offers a spot from which you can view the garden as a whole.

Bird Alert: See SFA Mast Arboretum.

Tour Policy: To arrange a tour for your group, call 936-468-1832.

Volunteer and Support Opportunities: To find out how you can help, call 936-468-1832. They're waiting to hear from you.

Driving Instructions: Loop 224 circles the city of Nacogdoches, so you can reach it easily no matter which way you come into town. Turn east on the loop. When you reach University Drive, turn north if you came into town from the south; turn south if you came into town from the north. Watch for the William R. Johnson Coliseum on the west side of the street. Pull in there to park, and walk up to the street; turn south and you'll be in the gardens. If you're going to spend the day here or be a frequent visitor, check with the University Police on College Street for a visitor's permit.

Stephen F. Austin State University Pineywoods Native Plant Center

Lady Bird Johnson Demonstration Garden
2900 Raguet Street
P.O. Box 13000 SFA Station
Nacogdoches, Texas 75962-3000
409-468-4600

Fee: Free.

Accessibility: Good to fair in the demonstration garden.

Days and Hours: Open weekdays during daylight hours.

Garden Type: Native plant demonstration garden and teaching and research facility in early stages of development.

Garden Size: A few hundred square feet planted in the Demonstration Garden. Trails are being built and plantings installed over eight acres. The property consists of almost 40 acres, but it is being developed in stages.

Themes and Special Features: Part of the University's Forest Resources Institute, this area will serve the intellectual and educational needs of students, scientists, and scholars seeking to protect forest ecosystems and understand the role humans play in their long-term future.

The Gardens: This is yet a young project, with ambitious plans to develop an educational facility centered on plants native to the region. Eventually, the founders will build greenhouses, an interpretive center, a nature trail, and a botanical garden of native plants. The small Lady Bird Johnson wildflower planting is a very good start.

Bird Alert: See SFA Mast Arboretum.

Volunteer and Support Opportunities: This project exists largely through grants and contributions from individuals, foundations, corporations, and public funds. If you're interested in helping to support this work, contact David Creech at 936-468-4343 or Barbara Stump at 936-468-3705.

Driving Instructions: Loop 224 circles the city of Nacogdoches, so you will see it, no matter which way you come into town. Turn east on the loop. When you reach University Drive, turn north if you came into town from the south; turn south if you came into town from the north. From University Drive, turn west on Austin and then south on Raguet Street. Watch on the left for a rough driveway turning into the woods. If you miss it, take the next one in front of the Forest Institutes sign.

Orange

Pinehurst Garden

Old Highway 90
P.O. Box 459
Orange, Texas 77631 (see Driving Instructions below)
409-883-5351
Orange Chamber of Commerce
409-883-3536; 800-528-4906

 **Fee:** Free.

Accessibility: Varies; call for details.

Days and Hours: Open to the public during the Daylily Festival the last two weekends in May, 9-5 Saturdays and 12-5 Sundays. Members of the American Hemerocallis Society may visit weekdays from May 15 through June 15.

Garden Type: Private estate created by daylily hybridizers to showcase their creations.

Garden Size: Two acres of daylilies set within a twenty-acre garden.

Themes and Special Features: This garden should be called "the Glory of Spring." Spring-blooming wonders—azalea, camellia, tulip, daffodil, hyacinth, and other early bloomers are quickly followed by three months of daylilies and other colorful perennials, like Asiatic lilies and irises, for a months-long celebration of the glories of spring. There is a topiary garden to admire if you tire of the endless seas of color, a bog garden, an aviary, a reflecting pool, and various water features.

Photos courtesy Pinehurst Garden

The Gardens: A private garden set amidst 100-year-old pine trees, Pinehurst houses what may be the largest collection of daylilies in the American South. Hybridizers Edgar and Betty Brown created the garden to display not only the 700 varieties they produced and named themselves, but also 1,000 of the best of their contemporaries' efforts and more than 100,000 specimens planted throughout the two-acre grounds.

Don't-Miss Feature: The topiary garden in the shape of a giant chessboard.

Bird Alert: Besides the aviary on the grounds, birds found in the vicinity include pine warbler, pileated, red-bellied, and downy woodpeckers.

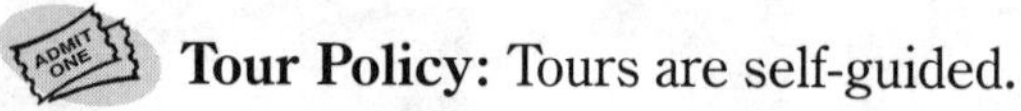

Tour Policy: Tours are self-guided.

Driving Instructions: From IH-10 from Houston, take Exit 874A for U.S. Business Highway 90, which will veer off to the right from the access road. Once over the railroad tracks, you've got about a mile and a half to go. Watch for the estate on the right.

On IH-10 from Louisiana, take the exit for Martin Luther King Drive, loop over the Interstate, and go south about a mile to U.S. Business Highway 90. Turn right and look for the estate on your left within a couple of hundred yards.

Tyler

Azalea and Spring Flower Trail

Tyler Area Chamber of Commerce,
Convention and Visitor Bureau
315 N. Broadway
Tyler, Texas 75702
800-235-5712
email: info@tylertexas.com
http://www.tylertexas.com

 **Fee:** Free

Accessibility: Will vary considerably; much can be seen from a driving tour.

Days and Hours: During daylight hours for a two-week period, usually the last week of March through the first week of April. I recommend that you call the Chamber to find out when peak bloom is expected in a given year, since it varies somewhat.

Garden Type: It's a self-guided tour, but you're going to want to have one of the pretty brochures with a map of the trail provided by the sponsors. A sure place to pick one up is the Convention and Visitor Bureau at 315 N. Broadway.

Garden Size: You will be driving and walking through eight miles of old residential districts on both sides of Broadway. Watch for signs and follow them. They will make your life a lot simpler. Traffic conditions can get pretty complicated, so you may need to plan to make more than one tour, with a different designated driver each time watching the road while the rest of you gawk.

Themes and Special Features: Although they are by no means the only source of color, azaleas take top awards as the showstoppers here. The area's sandy, acid soil has proven the ideal medium for them since their introduction to the area in 1929 by the landscape artist Maurice Shamburger, who imported them from the humus-rich woodlands of Alabama.

The Gardens: This public display of gardens makes my list of personal favorites, not only because it's incredibly beautiful during its spring heyday each year, but because it's the first such planting I ever saw, at the age of twenty.

I grew up in the western regions of the state. I'd seen the Piney Woods on annual visits to my father's family in Morris County and thus knew what a dogwood was and what a tulip magnolia looked like. I even had a hint as to the nature of azaleas—great blazes of warm colors that popped up for a few weeks wherever the soil was acid enough. But nothing I had ever seen had prepared me for the Spring Azalea Trail in Tyler when I discovered it in the early sixties, probably within a year or two of its first being opened to the public.

It was like a gourmet cook's discovering French food for the first time—a revelation of what miracles could be worked using natural materials and sweat.

The phenomenon you have here is not a single garden, of course. It is a panorama of flowering shrubs, vines, and dogwoods, and annual and perennial beds that spill and flow from one private yard to another, uniting the neighborhood into a single spectacle of bloom for two to three weeks in the spring. It's made up of shaded paths and sturdy little footbridges, ancient oaks and other native trees, every annual or perennial that can be coaxed into bloom at this time of year, and always and everywhere azaleas, great dazzling banks of azaleas, seas of azaleas, serried ranks and flotillas of azaleas. It's a sight that will bring you back year after year.

Most folks will want to start their tour from the courthouse on North Broadway and follow the Azalea Trail signs south. An 1898 Queen Anne-style mansion, an 1890s farmhouse, Greek Revival-style homes, 1930s-era homes, and just recently, 1970s-era homes provide the backdrop for this elegant celebration of springtime beauty. Don't be surprised if you're greeted by a lovely young woman in an antebellum getup and a dazzling smile. She's one of the Azalea Belles, official greeters serving on the weekends to help move visitors along and make your tour more enjoyable.

Don't-Miss Feature: My favorite site is the sunken garden at 212 Dobbs Street.

Sponsored Activities: This is a serious festival. The Azalea District's park fills up with vendors, historic old houses open their doors for guided tours, and antique shows and sales abound. There will be a quilt display, dances, concerts, fun runs, candlelight parties, and on and on. A premier event.

Tour Policy: Tours of the gardens are self-guided. Home tours will provide guides inside the houses.

Volunteer and Support Opportunities: Contact the Chamber of Commerce or Convention and Visitors Bureau at 800-235-5712.

Driving Instructions: Broadway is a major thoroughfare running north and south. It is also U.S. Highway 69. You can't miss it.

Breedlove Nursery

11576 State Highway 65 West
Tyler, Texas 75704-6930
903-597-7421

Fee: Free.

Accessibility: Variable in different areas; good in the retail and formal garden sections.

Days and Hours: 8-5:30 Monday-Saturday; 9-5 Sunday.

Garden Type: Display gardens at retail nursery.

Garden Size: About four acres in all, including retail area; three small display gardens.

Themes and Special Features: Knot garden, cottage garden, formal garden.

The Gardens: This is a good place to see how more formal, European elements may be incorporated into a Texas setting, for while the woodsy cottage garden and wisteria arbors are spectacular in early spring, it is the structure lent by the more traditional garden forms that maintains interest here year round. Native pines, oaks, and sweet gums shade rigidly clipped and shaped hedges and ivy trellises, where classic rectangular planting beds are laid out with brick paths along with a formal rose arbor, a pond with bubbling fountain, and a destination bench at one end of the garden.

A Victorian Knot Garden shows the quaint and really quite attractive idea of clipping small-leaved hedges, like box or yaupon, at different heights to make them look intertwined around a centerpiece, such as an armillary sundial.

Everything is on a small scale here and exquisitely proportioned. You'll find a touch of old-world formality mixed with southern tradition in the midst of the fragrant East Texas forest, making for a very pleasant place to spend an hour.

Don't-Miss Feature: Breedlove's has long set the standards for elegance in the home landscape in a city noted for elegant landscapes. Formality expressed in parterres and knot gardens is very much a part of the heritage of Texas gardens, despite the modern turn toward more casual expressions in home landscapes and public plantings. Breedlove's preserves that flavor of old gardens that is sometimes described as "English," sometimes as "Old South," and always as "refined" in the products sold here—a selection of pots, sundials, topiaries, and statuary to dress the formal garden. Check it out.

Bird Alert: In this part of the state, you can expect the woods to be full of birds all year long. In winter, yellow-bellied sapsucker may visit the trees, while kinglets, both golden-crowned and red-crowned, may be flitting among them. Pine siskin, dark-eyed junco, hermit thrush, and red-breasted nuthatch may put in a showing.

Driving Instructions: Drive west from Tyler on Highway 65 until you're just out of town. You'll think you've missed it, but stay alert. You'll see it on the north (right) side of the road.

Municipal Rose Garden

1900 West Front Street (or 420 S. Rose Park)
Tyler, Texas 75702
903-531-1213
Rose Museum: 903-597-3130
email: info@tylertexas.com
http://www.tylertexas.com

Fee: Free for garden and garden center; small admission charged for Rose Museum.

Accessibility: Excellent.

Days and Hours: Garden open daily during daylight hours. Garden Center open daily 8-5, Sunday 1-4. Closed on major holidays. Rose Museum open 9-5 Tuesday through Friday, 10-5 on Saturday, and 1:30-5 on Sunday. Closed on major holidays.

Garden Type: Dedicated rose garden for public display and research.

Garden Size: Fourteen acres. With some 38,000 to 40,000 specimens of more than 500 varieties, mostly modern, this is one of, if not the largest, collection of roses open to the public in the whole world.

Themes and Special Features: One acre is devoted to heritage roses and a Sensory Garden. There are also xeriscape and perennial displays.

The Gardens: This garden sits in the heart of rose country. A fifth of all commercial rose production in the United States takes place right here in Smith County. And since most commercial rose production is focused on hybrid tea and other modern roses, that's mostly what you will see here. Sited in straight-sided raised beds, row after magnificent row of color lights up even the dullest day through several months of the year. As many as 2,000 plants will be replaced in a year's time in a fierce effort to keep the garden always at its best. April and May and then September and October offer the grandest show. If you love modern roses, you will be drawn here again and again because this is where you come to see what specimens will look like in your own landscape.

The Museum: The Rose Museum was created to preserve and display the history of one of the area's most vital economic assets—the roses grown in its sandy fields and shipped all over the world. Here you will find mementos such as the jeweled gowns of former queens of the Rose Festival, dating from the thirties, to a state-of-the-art computer system for cataloguing and identifying roses.

The gift shop features everything under the sun related to roses—from dried hips to scented pillows, daintily painted teacups to posters and books—making this one of the downright prettiest, and prettiest smelling, gift shops you're ever likely to enter. Don't miss it.

Sponsored Activities: A conference and seminar on growing roses is held in winter each year. Contact the garden center for a current schedule.

Related Event: One of the state's premier public festivals takes place in Tyler during the third week of October each year—the Texas Rose Festival. Since 1933 folks have been flocking into the city each fall to celebrate the rose. Today crowds swell to over 100,000 during the five-day event, while parades, art shows, crafts fairs, flower displays, and musical events crowd the days leading up to the presentation of the Rose Queen and her Court. Beautiful young women—the flower of Texas womanhood, it's been said—wear ravishing gowns and ride on floats and entertain the public as "Rose Royalty." It's quite a sight to see.

Tour and Rental Policy: Tours of the garden are self-guided. The garden center can be rented for weddings, anniversaries, and other celebrations.

Volunteer and Support Opportunities: Contact the garden at the number above.

Driving Instructions: Front Street runs east and west from one side of town to the other. It is also State Highway 31. From it on the west side of town, turn south onto Rose Park between Loop 323 and U.S. Highway 69. There's a huge parking lot. If you get lost, anyone in town can direct you to "the Rose Garden."

Finding More Flowers in East Texas

Beaumont

The Council of Garden Clubs coordinates a tour of private gardens on the first weekend in May. For this year's details, call 409-842-3135.

Mount Pleasant

A charming, five-acre private garden to explore during spring and summer is Tankersley Gardens. Call 903-572-0567 for a schedule and directions.

Nacogdoches

Daylily display gardens endorsed by the American Hemerocallis Society will be open to the public during certain days in late spring or early summer. Call Jean and Kathy Barnhart at 936-564-2920.

Victoria

A weekend in March is set aside for touring private gardens in this enchanting old town. Trinity Episcopal School Board has charge. You can reach them at 361-573-3220.

Part Four

The Gardens of Central Texas

Austin, Brenham, Bryan/College Station, Dripping Springs, Fredericksburg, Georgetown, Harwood, Independence, Lampasas, Round Top, San Antonio

Sign on wildflower meadow fence:
"The bull can cross this pasture in 14.3 seconds. Can you?"

Wildflowers in general and bluebonnets in particular grace fields, ditches, roadsides, and open spaces all over Texas, but the Central Texas Hill Country wears the crown as the most popular area for wildflower viewing. There are four rules for enjoying them:

1. Stay off private property.
2. Stay off fire ant mounds.
3. Stay off rattlesnakes.
4. Have a nice day.

If you want to see the bluebonnets, come in early spring, from March through April. That's when fields all over the area turn into seas of color that mirror the clear blue of the open skies. Take a pass through Georgetown if you can, and see the poppies blooming at about the same time. Or, if you have a weekend to devote, plan to take in some of the popular wildflower driving routes or visit a state park or two. From Austin, drive west to check out areas around Llano, Johnson City, Fredericksburg, and Kerrville. Visit the Lyndon B. Johnson State and National Historical Parks, about 14 miles west of Johnson City. If you're going east, take State Highway 71 through Bastrop, La Grange, and Columbus. Washington County can be breathtaking, too. U.S. 281 North toward Marble Falls and Lampasas also offers spectacular views.

Many communities sponsor wildflower events, fests, and celebrations during this time. Georgetown celebrates the red poppy, Burnet and Chappell Hill throw a Bluebonnet Festival, and other communities offer attractions for the tourist. The Lady Bird Johnson Wildflower Center in Austin holds a Spring Gardening Festival in early April and a Plants and People Festival toward the end of the month.

Another rich display in early spring comes from the fruit trees. More peaches are produced in the Hill Country than anywhere else in the state, and here you will find the only attempts to grow apples on a commercial basis. Some of the pear trees brightening the very early spring woods are over 100 years old.

Because Mother Nature is unpredictable, it's impossible to say very far ahead when wildflower viewing will be at its peak in a particular area. Fortunately, the Texas Department of Transportation will keep you updated. Call 800-452-9292 as often as you wish to find out what is blooming where at any time.

The Department also reminds us not to trespass on private property in our transported state of wildflower enjoyment, not to damage anything on government property, either, such as highway right-of-way, and not to even think about digging up clumps of wildflowers. You can buy seeds for any species that's suitable for cultivation in the gift shop of just about any garden mentioned in this book.

If you want more information about growing your own wildflowers, including details about what will grow in other states, there are two excellent sources, the Lady Bird Johnson Wildflower Center in Austin and Wildseed Farms in Fredericksburg. See their listings below.

But if you miss the early spring show, don't despair. With a climate that provides up to 275 frost-free days each year and an annual rainfall from 30 to 40 inches, Central Texas rarely lacks for color along its roadsides. Paintbrush and blanketflower outlast the bluebonnets and are joined by Mexican hat, evening primrose, winecups, several kinds of bright yellow daisies, white daisies, wild phlox, blue mistflower, gayfeather, bindweed, and asters for color right up until hard frost. The tens of thousands of pounds of wildflower seeds sown along the roadside by the Texas Department of Transportation each year include up to thirty different varieties of blooming plants

You would expect such a bountiful heritage of flowering plants to lead to a burgeoning of public gardens in Central Texas, and indeed it has. Herbs often star in them, thriving in the drier reaches and producing some truly spectacular displays. Here you will find such Mediterranean heirlooms as lavender and prostrate rosemary growing lustily beside Mexican herbs like hoja santa and epazote and natives like bee balm and echinacea. You will see them being used as mainstays in the landscaping of homes, parks, and even business developments, and showcased in the public gardens. In San Antonio, the famous Riverwalk meanders past walls dripping with rosemary. In Fredericksburg, a whole retail nursery centers around nothing but herbs. In almost every garden you explore in this part of the state, herbs play a major role.

Roses, too, are happy to live in this area, especially the older cultivars known as "old roses," "heirloom roses," or "antique roses." Many sport German names, having been brought here in the nineteenth century by early settlers from Germany: Gruss an Aachen, Dortmund, Frau Karl Druschki, Veilchenblau, and many others.

This region is also home to one of the finest retail nurseries in the state and my own all-time-favorite Texas garden, The Antique Rose Emporium in Independence.

The most obvious roadside birds you will see as you drive the long highways in Central Texas include eastern and western kingbirds, American kestrel, red-tailed or red-shouldered hawk, Cooper's hawk, greater roadrunner, eastern bluebird, barn swallow, and great blue heron.

Austin

It's About Thyme

11726 Manchaca Road
Austin, Texas 78748
512-280-1192

 **Fee:** Free.

Accessibility: Good.

 **Days and Hours:** Open daily 8-6.

Garden Type: Display herb garden at retail nursery center.

Garden Size: Backyard size.

Themes and Special Features: Mexican, Old World, and Southwestern herbs and old roses.

The Gardens: Huge, healthy specimens of sweet bay, rosemary, mint marigold, and salvias of many varieties grow so exuberantly here that they spill out of their beds and block the gravel pathway by late summer. A friendly tabby greeted me on my last visit and explored the fragrant beds at my side.

Don't-Miss Feature: One of the largest hoja santa plants I've ever seen.

Bird Alert: Orchard oriole and red-bellied woodpecker are possible in this metropolitan but wooded area.

Gift Shop: A 120-year-old house holds the well-stocked gift shop, where you'll find a selection of reasonably priced garden art and gifts. Five greenhouses yield an astonishing variety of herbs for sale.

Driving Instructions: From IH-35 take Slaughter Lane west to Manchaca Road and turn south (left). Drive about five miles and look for the nursery on the right.

Lady Bird Johnson Wildflower Center

4801 La Crosse Avenue
Austin, Texas 78739-1702
512-292-4100
http://www.wildflower.org

Fee: Adults $5; Students and Seniors $4; Children four and younger free; Members free.

Accessibility: Good throughout, except on the nature trails. Some wheelchairs are available in the Visitors Gallery.

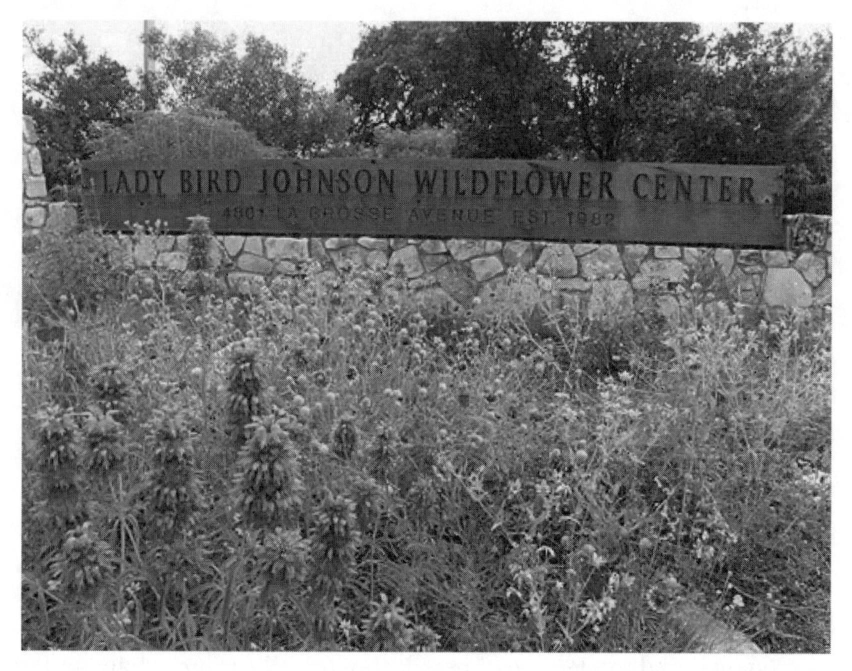

Photo by Ronald Sprouse

Days and Hours: Open 9-5:30 Tuesday through Sunday; shorter hours for the Visitors Gallery, café, and nature store. Closed Mondays and major holidays.

Garden Type: Perfectly adapted to its environment, this display garden educates the public in the use and utility of regional plants.

Garden Size: Many small, cultivated beds, including 23 theme gardens, as well as a couple of ¼-mile nature trails and a wildflower meadow.

Organic Maintenance: Mosquito larvae in the rainwater cisterns are controlled with a naturally occurring bacterium called *Bacillus thuringiensis israelensis*, which harms nothing else.

Themes and Special Features: Everything here, from the parking lot and pathways to a vast rainwater collection system, is planned and

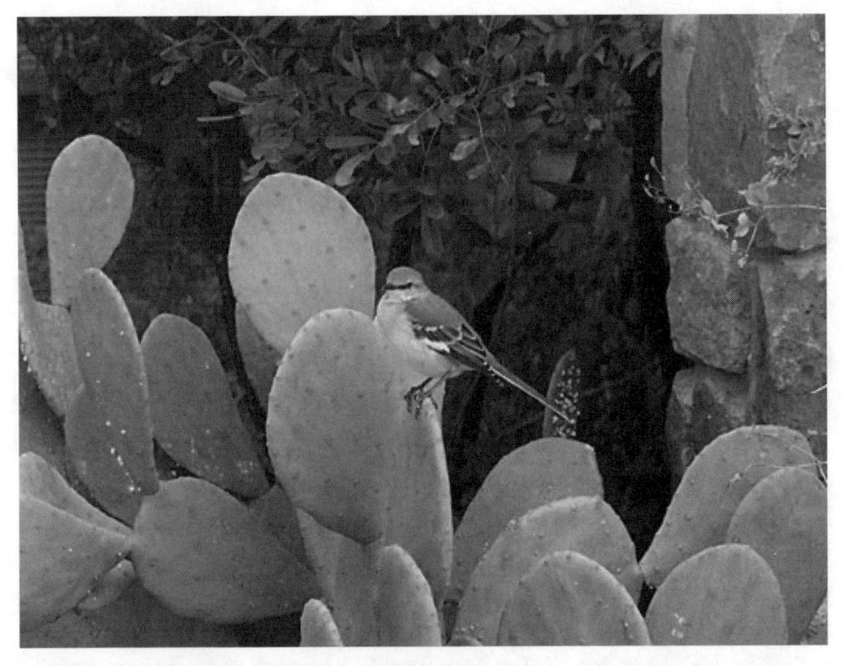

Photo by Ronald Sprouse

executed to showcase regional resources, trees, flowers, stones, and water. The beautiful white stone used as building material throughout the grounds comes from local quarries. Buildings boast passive solar heating and zoned air conditioning in support of the center's low-impact-on-the-ecosystem philosophy. Recycled materials and paints and adhesives selected for lack of toxicity played a big part in construction. And the Center's water needs are supplemented by the largest rooftop system for collecting and distributing rainwater in all of North America.

Displays include two dozen theme gardens, each planned to showcase the uses of native plants. Among the most intriguing theme gardens are those featuring Deer Resistant Plants; Red, White and Blue Plants; Plants to Attract Songbirds; Prairie Grasses; Healing Plants; and White Plants. A wildflower meadow steals the limelight in spring and early summer.

The Visitor Gallery features exhibits illustrating native plants that can be used for food, medicine, and landscaping.

Garden Recognition: The property has earned certification as a Backyard Wildlife Habitat from the National Wildlife Federation and is a Texas Wildscape Demonstration Site for the Texas Parks and Wildlife Department.

The Gardens: Set in a natural (you might even say wild) environment only minutes from the heart of the state's capital city, this garden serves as a testament to the interest growing statewide in the beauty and utility of native plant species. The folks here want to show off the natural beauty of Texas, but their ultimate goal is to demonstrate to regional homeowners some of the choices available for landscaping properties without stressing scarce resources like water.

Well-marked paths lead you so smoothly through the grounds that you may never realize you're being educated, as you wander past display beds dedicated to native mustang grapes, muse among the old roses, and rest on one of the comfortable benches placed thoughtfully throughout the arbored spaces to provide shade when you need it most.

Photo by Ronald Sprouse

The Home Comparison Gardens illustrate two different approaches to landscaping with native plants. Buffalo grass forms the center of the Formal Design display, bordered with perennial beds of mannerly salvias and other shrubs. The Informal Design shows a landscape that can be kept looking natural, but with its wildness under enough control to satisfy your neighbors. A bonus for both designs is their attractiveness to the native fauna that we find most delightful—butterflies, hummingbirds, and songbirds.

Don't-Miss Feature: In the middle of the paved courtyard, you will discover a replica of a Hill Country limestone pool full of clear, deep water. It reminds you not only how precious water is, but how beautiful, too.

Sponsored Activities: The public loves this place. You can see it on their faces as they stroll the grounds, often with cameras or notebooks in hand, enthralled by the possibilities for transforming their own thirsty, demanding yards into environmentally sound ecosystems in harmony with their settings. But it's the native plant and seed sales, held in spring and fall, that reveal the true depth of the public's willingness to "go native." The sales are so popular that parking lots fill up, and the center has to run a shuttle bus from a nearby high school lot to accommodate the shoppers.

They have a whole Education Department here to handle the demand for classes, conferences, children's programming, and teacher training. Call for a current schedule or become a member and get advance notification of events.

Bird Alert: This place is so popular during spring and summer that the only birds you're likely to encounter are those adapted to urban living who have little or no fear of human beings, like house sparrows, grackles, and other blackbirds. But the surrounding woods are natural habitat for many birds throughout the year, so keep an eye out. You might spot a western scrub-jay, house finch, or lesser gold finch in the winter, a blue grosbeak or orchard oriole in the summer.

Tour and Rental Policies: Tours are both self-guided and docent-guided, and group rates are available. You will need reservations for anything but the self-guided tour. Call 512-292-4200.

Classrooms and the auditorium are available for rental both day and night. Other buildings and the grounds themselves are available for evening events, with certain restrictions. Call the Facility Sales office at 512-292-4200.

Volunteer and Support Opportunities: Volunteer programs here offer the opportunity to support the Center, no matter what your area of expertise. They will put you to work conducting tours, propagating plants, stocking merchandise in the gift store, planning special projects, or answering phones and greeting visitors. And if you have a talent they haven't yet thought of putting to use, they want to talk to you. Pick up a Volunteer Information brochure in the Visitors Gallery, or request one from the address above.

As for donations, well, since the Center draws no operating funds from any government entity, it depends on memberships, donations, and contributions to keep going. Membership costs from $25 to $50 and brings you special rates on classes and the gift shop, along with a subscription to the newsletter and admission to members-only events, like the preview sales that precede the public sales of plants and seeds. Your membership card is also honored at many other botanical institutes, saving you admission fees in places like the San Antonio Botanical Garden, for instance. Pick up an application form at the Visitors Gallery or write to the address above to request one.

Gift Shop: Reserve a few moments while you're here to visit Wild Ideas: The Store, one of the best-stocked art-and-nature stores anywhere in the state. It keeps the same hours as the grounds, except for Sundays, when it is open only from 1-4.

A delightful small café, called predictably enough, The Wildflower Café, provides a tasty light lunch or dessert. It's open 10-4 Tuesday through Saturday, 11-4 on Sunday.

Driving Instructions: The Wildflower Center is easy to find. La Crosse Avenue crosses MoPac Expressway on the south side of the city. Turn east (there's a sign with an arrow to point the way) and drive right up to the parking lot.

Mayfield Park Garden

3801 Old Bull Creek Road
Austin, Texas 78703
Austin Parks and Recreation Department
Administration: 512-974-6700
Facilities Reservations: 512-474-9692

Fee: Free.

Accessibility: Good.

Days and Hours: Open daily during daylight hours.

Garden Type: A public park with both natural woodlands and landscaped gardens, including a herb garden.

Garden Size: Twenty-three acres of parkland, not all cultivated.

Themes and Special Features: Native plants include mountain laurel and turk's cap, very attractive to hummingbirds in late summer and fall. Landscaping in cultivated areas reflects the plants that would have been found in this area during the 1930s and 1940s.

The Gardens: Volunteers plant and maintain the different gardens. Of particular interest is the beautiful herb garden cared for by the very active Austin Herb Society. Lily ponds and palm trees also add to the park-like atmosphere.

Don't-Miss Feature: Peacocks parade proudly through the grounds. You will probably hear their raucous calls long before you see the birds, but don't miss the chance for a close-up view. A male peacock's spread feathers glinting in the sunlight is one of the world's most magnificent sights.

Bird Alert: In the oak-juniper woodlands, look for ladder-backed woodpecker and yellow-billed cuckoo during the summer. Black-chinned and ruby-throated hummingbirds will be visiting the flowers. Year-round residents may include northern flicker or yellow-bellied sapsucker. Soaring overhead may be sharp-shinned or Cooper's hawks.

Sponsored Activities: Austin Herb Society holds regular meetings with outstanding programs that are open to the public for a small fee. It also co-sponsors with the Austin Area Garden Club an annual Herb Fest in the fall. Membership in the organization brings added benefits, including access to study-group meetings, seed and cutting exchanges, field trips, and various discounts. You may contact the Austin Herb Society through Zilker Botanical Gardens at 512-477-8672.

Tour and Rental Policies: Tours are self-guided. The 1870s cottage and its grounds are available for workshops, retreats, and small parties. All Austin park facilities are extremely popular venues and must be reserved up to seven months in advance. For details, visit the web site or call the Austin Parks Department at 512-474-9692.

Volunteer and Support Opportunities: Contact the Austin Herb Society through Zilker Botanical Gardens at 512-477-8672.

Driving Instructions: The historic park and landscaped grounds are located next to the Laguna Gloria Museum of Art on 35th Street. Turn west from the MoPac Expressway onto West 35th and follow the signs.

The Natural Gardener

8648 Old Bee Caves Road
Austin, Texas 78735
512-288-6113
email: information@naturalgardeneraustin.com
http://www.naturalgardeneraustin.com

 **Fee:** Free.

Accessibility: Excellent.

 **Days and Hours:** Open 8-6 Monday through Saturday, Sunday 10-5. Closes an hour earlier during winter months.

Garden Type: Display gardens at retail nursery: herb, vegetable, ornamental beds, a butterfly garden, and a labyrinth.

Photo courtesy The Natural Gardener

Garden Size: Two acres of display; six acres of retail, laid out in such natural settings as to make the sales area look like a garden, too.

Organic Maintenance: All organic.

Themes and Special Features: Here you will find the author's favorite herb garden in all of Texas, designed by herb specialist, cook, and author Lucinda Hutson.

The Gardens: The gardens here are simple but clever—an absolutely stunning marketing tool for showing off products and processes. It's organic gardening that owner John Dromgoole sells here, along with the widest possible selection of herbs, vegetables, flowers, shrubs, and trees that can be grown regionally without synthetic chemicals or other toxins. The gardens show his customers how it's done. Lima beans spill over neat trellises, tomatoes fight their cages, and a nine-foot tower of malabar spinach dominates the vegetable garden. The Herb Garden shows just how beautiful herbs in the landscape can be, but its heart is its culinary genius. Mexican herbs

Photos courtesy The Natural Gardener

hold the garden's perimeter, with Mediterranean, Provençal, and southeast Asian herbs in their own beds within the circle. Huge rosemaries vie for attention beside nopal cactus and yucca. Lavender, African blue basil, oregano, sage, mint marigold, chives, and garlic chives invite the cook to get the pot boiling. It's time to start supper.

The Butterfly Garden is another best-of-kind, laid out neatly to show off the beauty of perennials, grasses, and herbs. Fight your way through the butterflies to see what thrives here. Caryopteris, dianthus, zexmenia, coreopsis, black dalea, showy sedum, aster, rain lily, Russian sage—how can so much color be packed into such a small area? I saw things here that I've never seen in another public garden, such as skeleton-leaf goldeneye, woody butterfly bush, and yellow pavonia. And best of all, I didn't have to guess what they were. Neat, legible signs identified everything for me.

Don't-Miss Feature: There are always animals about here. A black cat named "Guano," dogs looking for an adoptive home, even burros in a pasture behind the gardens. Children love to feed the hens and rooster at the chicken house.

Bird Alert: Black-chinned hummingbird may be seen busily pollinating the flowers. If you see a flash of bright red, it may be either northern cardinal or summer tanager.

Sponsored Activities: Classes, workshops, and sponsored speakers are considered an important part of customer service. Events are frequent and usually free. You can get a schedule by calling the number above.

Tour Policy: Group tours are easy to arrange. Just call ahead.

Gift Shop: The whole place is a store. Pottery, yard art, organic growing supplies, and gifty gardening stuff round out the top-notch selection of plants.

Driving Instructions: Pay attention, now. This place can be a challenge to find, but it's well worth the effort. Take the phone number with you just in case.

From downtown Austin, take the MoPac Expressway south to the Southwest Parkway exit. Go west (right) on the parkway 4.5 miles (check the odometer) and turn south (left) onto Travis Cook Road. After about half a mile, this road dead ends at Old Bee Caves Road. Look for the nursery on the right.

Coming from the south, take IH-35 north to the exit for U.S. Highways 290 and 71 West. Go west into Oak Hill. Where the highways split, stay to the right on 71 West. After about one mile, turn right on Fletcher. It shortly dead ends at Old Bee Caves Road. Turn left and go about ½ to ¾ mile. You will find The Natural Gardener on your right. Get out and give yourself the treat you deserve by taking a tour of the herb garden.

If you are using a map to try to figure this out, please note that there is more than one Bee Caves Road. You want the "Old" one in Oak Hill.

Zilker Botanical Garden

2220 Barton Springs Road
Austin, Texas 78746
512-477-8672
http://www.zilkergarden.org

Austin Parks & Recreation Department

Fee: Free; donations welcomed.

Accessibility: Varies considerably. Call 512-478-6875 for information.

Days and Hours: Grounds are open every day from dawn to dusk. Hours for the Visitor Center and Gift Shop vary.

Garden Type: Botanical garden with a rich variety of trees, shrubs, flowers, and water features.

Garden Size: Twenty-two acres.

Themes and Special Features: Oriental Garden, gardens devoted to herbs, fragrance, roses, daylilies, cacti, and succulents. Xeriscape

Demonstration Garden. A Pioneer Settlement features a vegetable and fruit garden. A limestone quarry preserves tracks and fossils from the early Cretaceous period in the Hartman Prehistoric Garden.

The Gardens: I'm a sucker for the oriental touch in a Texas garden. The contrast is just so delicious. And the expressions so individual. You might think all oriental-inspired gardens would have a tiresome sameness about them, but nothing could be further from the truth. They express the visions of individual gardeners with an incredible range of imagination, from unrestrained exuberance to focused formality.

The Isamu Taniguchi Garden tucked into a caliche hillside within the Zilker shows a rugged character in total contrast to the smoothness of many other such gardens. It puts the uneven grounds to exquisite use in a series of small waterfalls and lily ponds along a stony stream that meanders down to a large pond full of fat orange koi. Water lilies bloom from the middle of June until October, and boulders, tree trunks, and shrubs clipped into bonsai-like shapes show up in a subtle interplay of light and shadow. In the pond, carefully placed stepping stones lead the intrepid across to a boat-shaped island to the pleasure of little boys of all ages.

But the Taniguchi is only one of several delights awaiting you here. The Mabel Davis Rose Garden offers a look at antique roses, as well as the latest All-America selections, while the Butterfly Trail swarms in April and October with butterflies of every description lured there by the plants selected to appeal to the widest number of species. Butterfly feeders supplement the natural food, and the air seems alive with softly fluttering wings.

The Zilker Botanical Garden reflects the era in which it was born, more than half a century ago, in its stone-set-in-concrete walks and walls, its silted ponds, and fifty-year-old garden benches. Lovingly maintained and obviously very popular with the community, it emits a quiet kind of nostalgia that appeals to all ages. The Rose Garden remains a favorite spot for weddings, and you'll always find young

Photos courtesy Zilker Botanical Garden

couples wandering the shady paths hand in hand. In fact, half a million folks a year sample the enjoyments found here.

In March and April, the Hamilton Parr Memorial Azalea Garden puts on a first-class show, and the Daylily Garden created by the Austin Hemerocallis Society glows in spring and early summer. That's also a good time to catch the blooms in the Cactus and Succulent Garden.

I find the Pioneer Settlement Gardens particularly interesting, with their plantings of papaya, mango, starfruit, Mexican lime, and taro mixed in among the okra, tomato, eggplant, runner beans, and chard.

Don't-Miss Feature: Well, of course, it's the Dinosaur Garden. Hundred-million-year-old tracks and bones don't crop up in every garden you tour. Here, they form the underpinnings of an exhibit that is the latest addition to the Zilker. When completed, this garden will recreate a time when dinosaurs roamed among gingko trees and ferns to leave their tracks in the boggy flats. Epiphytes and bromeliads contribute to the tropical feel, and a paleontologist's reconstructed dig site reaffirms the authenticity of the discovery. Kids will love it.

And don't miss the Herb and Fragrance Garden, where you will find such unusual and powerfully fragrant herbs as patchouli and Old Spice-scented geranium.

Bird Alert: Zilker Park is home to hundreds of bird species, some highly colorful like summer tanager and northern oriole, others more retiring, like golden-cheeked warbler or red-bellied woodpecker. During spring and fall migrations, many warbler species pass through town. Early morning birding excursions can be very rewarding here.

Sponsored Activities: Free educational tours lead school children through the gardens throughout the year. A Herb Festival in October and Garden Festival in April headline the many, many events hosted or held here. Sales of cactus and succulents, African violets, irises, gourds, and bulbs alternate with shows of everything from chrysanthemums to ikebana. There is always something going on here. Pick up a schedule in the Visitor Center or call for information.

Tour and Rental Policies: Educational tours for school children are free, arranged through the schools. You can arrange a tour for adults for $2 a head, but the garden needs a minimum of $25, so, if your group isn't big enough, maybe a small donation would offset its size. Call 512-481-8256.

Special occasions, including weddings, can be scheduled from April through November for a small usage fee. Make your reservations early by calling 512-474-9692.

Volunteer and Support Opportunities: Some forty garden clubs contribute time, effort, money, and imagination to maintaining and enhancing these gardens. Volunteers are also sought to act as greeters for visitors, work in the educational programs, and do the myriad little things it takes to keep a facility like this in show attire. Call 512-477-8672 to talk about what you can offer. Membership in the Friends of the Zilker Botanical Garden starts at $50, but if you join at a level of $100 or more, you can have a brick inscribed with your name or a memorial and placed in the Garden's Walk of Friends. Membership also nets you a 10 percent discount in the gift shop for a year.

Gift Shop: A small gift shop inside the Austin Area Garden Center offers a selection of books and other gifts that, while limited, is tastefully chosen.

Driving Instructions: The Zilker Botanical Garden is located within Zilker Park south of the city lakes formed by the Colorado River. You can access Barton Springs Road from the MoPac Expressway north or south, and drive east. Watch for signs.

Brenham

Ellison's Greenhouses, Inc.

1808 Horton
Brenham, Texas 77833
979-836-0084; 979-836-6011

Fee: A small admission fee is charged for the greenhouse tour and special events.

Accessibility: The shop is fully accessible. Call for details about tours.

Days and Hours: Nursery open Monday-Friday 9-5, Saturday 9-3, Sundays seasonally. See Tour Policy below for times when the greenhouses may be visited.

Garden Type: Retail nursery and commercial greenhouses, offering tours to the public.

Garden Size: About five acres of greenhouses.

The Garden: The attraction here is the chance to see working greenhouses in operation, producing masses of bloom. According to season, you will see thousands upon thousands of such colorful flowers as poinsettias, hydrangeas, and lilies, as well as a wide assortment of foliage plants for indoor use.

Sponsored Activities: Each year in November, Ellison's stages the Annual Poinsettia Celebration, a spectacular two-day event featuring as many as 80,000 blooming poinsettias, with musical and other entertainments, food vendors, demonstrations on plant care, and activities for the kids. Some of the proceeds from ticket sales are donated to local charities.

Photos courtesy Ellison's Greenhouse

Tour Policy: Tours of the greenhouses for individuals or groups may be scheduled Monday through Thursday by calling the number above. If you're there on a Friday or Saturday, reservations aren't required. Friday tours begin at 10:00, 11:00, 1:00, and 3:00. Saturday they begin at 11:00 and 1:00 only.

Gift Shop: Full-line nursery and gift items, lovely foliage plants, and hanging baskets.

Driving Instructions: From downtown Brenham, drive west on Alamo and turn south (right) on Horton Street. Look for Ellison's Nursery on your right just before you reach Stone Street.

Bryan-College Station

Texas A&M University Horticultural Gardens

Dr. Don Wilkerson
Department of Horticultural Sciences
Texas A&M University
College Station, Texas 77843-2134
(see Driving Instructions below)
979-845-5341
http://www.aggie-horticulture.tamu.edu/greenhouse/new/gate/intro.html

Fee: Free.

Accessibility: Mostly very good, but varies some. Wood-chip paths offer about an eighth of a mile of strolling. Shaded benches are now being placed every 100 feet. A paved road through the heart of the garden offers good views from the car.

Days and Hours: Open every day from dawn to dusk.

Garden Type: These showy gardens are planted and maintained by students pursuing degrees in horticulture. Here they learn and practice skills in plant and turf care, landscaping, greenhouse and nursery growing, and grounds maintenance. They have fun doing it, and it shows.

Garden Size: Fifteen acres, with over 1,000 plant specimens in habitats ranging from bog gardens to desert lands. Most individual beds are not large, but intelligent design and intensive planting give a lush appearance.

The 20,000-square-foot container nursery and 6,000-square-foot greenhouse are for university use only and not open to the public.

Themes and Special Features: The need to provide hands-on experience to the next generation of landscape and garden managers shapes activities here. Beds stay in flux as new classes form and take over the work left by the last. On a recent visit, I saw an eye-popping experiment in using gray and gray-blue foliage plants as focal points in color beds, complimenting yellow, pink, and blue flowers.

Your pets can come with you here, assuming you're willing to follow the guidelines for keeping them leashed and under control. You'll also have to "stoop and scoop" to clean up any waste. See the Guidelines posted in the kiosk at the parking area.

The Gardens: When you leave your car in the parking lot, look for the kiosk near the entrance to the facility. They call this the Howdy Haus. Here you will find announcements of upcoming events, as well as the first of many visitor-aids to guide you through the gardens. These are laminated fact sheets, full of information about what you're seeing at each step along the way. Take the time to scan each one and then return it to its container for the next person to pick up and use.

You'll quickly see that the garden is designed to provide the widest range of experiences possible in a limited space. Individual beds keep their unique identities, even as they blend into a whole that makes for a pleasant time for the visitor. Plants here look comfortable in their spaces, beginning with the Ornamental Grass area near the parking lot, where over 20 grass species show what they can lend to the landscape. Wander through the Hill Country Garden, the West Texas Garden, and all the others in between, admiring the roses, vines, and blooming perennials in all the beds.

Here you will find one of the best expositions of the use of herbs in the landscape, especially of the notoriously fussy gray beauty lavender, and experience the beauty of mature shrub roses like Belinda's Dream. This is one of the few gardens I've seen that make enough use of perennial native hibiscus and heat-loving cosmos. You'll delight in the "English Garden" effect achieved in the Texas Perennial Border by planting Texas natives in luxuriant drifts.

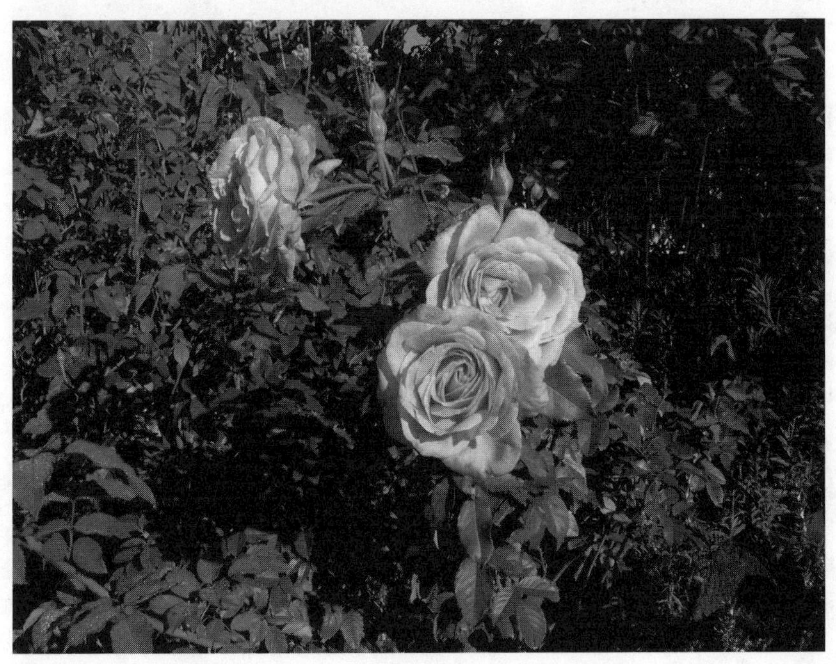

Don't-Miss Feature: The Lou Cashion Memorial Garden tucked into the southwest corner of the grounds embodies what to me is best about Texas gardens and does it on a delightfully miniature scale. A neat and colorful cottage-style combination of vegetables, herbs, and ornamentals enclosed by a simple fence and backed by a small vineyard, it's a sweet reminder of a time when people depended on private gardens to provide most of the staples of life as well as many of its pleasures.

Lavender plays a starring role here, anchoring a pedestaled sundial and backed by glistening, purple hyacinth bean. Mints grow as ground covers and sweet basil and cinnamon basil scent the air. Captivating.

Coming Soon: An extensive Crape Myrtle Trail is being installed. It will incorporate about 30 different varieties of these stars of the summer garden in a joint project with the civic organization Brazos Beautiful, Incorporated.

Bird Alert: This is a peaceful place, despite being tucked into a niche inside a busy mid-sized city. Carefully tended bird feeders keep feathered visitors coming in abundance, including tufted titmouse, ladder-backed woodpecker, and ruby-throated hummingbird. A skyward glance will often yield a red-tailed hawk.

Sponsored Activities: Classes, presentations, field trips, and children's activities are available seasonally. The Fall Plant Sale held in late October is a good reason to become a member. You get early access to the plants on sale and discounted admission to all events. Call 979-845-3658 to learn about scheduled events.

Volunteer and Support Opportunities: The TAMU Horticultural Garden doesn't depend on the university for its operating budget. It seeks out grants, donations, and membership programs and makes effective use of generous volunteers from the community. Memberships range from $20 to over $500. Ongoing funds that support new projects and student scholarships welcome your contribution. Or you can dedicate a bench or other feature as a tribute or memorial and leave a lasting effect on the garden. To volunteer or offer other contributions, call 979-845-3658.

Tour Policy: Self-guided tours are possible at any time, thanks to the markers along the paths and the handouts available at various stations along the way. A special Kid Stuff Guide has been developed to help teachers and youth leaders introduce children to over 20 terms relating to nature. Visitors can arrange a guided tour, but you'll need an appointment, since this is a working "classroom." Call 979-845-5341 for information.

Driving Instructions: State Highway 6 Business is one of the major north-south streets through College Station. It is also called Texas Avenue. Just north of its intersection with University Drive (FM 60), you will find a street called Hensel Drive that goes west from Texas Avenue. Turn here and watch for the TAMU Gardens on your right. There's ample parking in the lot.

If you get lost, you will find the Bryan/College Station Chamber of Commerce and Convention and Visitor's Bureau to be staffed with exceptionally friendly and helpful people. They'll give you a map and circle your destination for you. The office is at 715 University Drive E., and their number is 979-260-9898.

Dripping Springs

Pure Luck Organics/Pure Luck Grade A Goat Dairy

Pure Luck Texas
Farm and Diary

101 Twin Oaks Trail
Dripping Springs, Texas 78620
512-858-7034; 800-256-8268

email: pureluck@mindspring.com
http://www.purelucktexas.com

 **Fee:** Free.

Accessibility: Rough, but possible for some of the most colorful parts of the grounds.

 **Days and Hours:** This is private property, open Saturdays only.

Garden Type: Small, family-operated farm and dairy, specializing in organically grown fresh-cut herbs, flowers, and specialty vegetables, free-range eggs, and site-made natural goat cheese. The owners are Sara and Denny Bolton.

Garden Size: About eight acres, including a greenhouse and four large cold frames.

Organic Maintenance: Certified as totally organic by the Texas Department of Agriculture. Uses only natural products for fertilizer and pest and disease control.

Themes and Special Features: Do you like basil? Well, this place is a basil-lover's delight. Row upon row upon row of the stuff, in several different flavors, stand at the center of this family enterprise. There are plenty of other aromatic herbs, too, for admiring or for buying fresh-cut.

Like goat cheese? Sample some first-rate ones in the dairy's tiny tasting room. Pure Luck just keeps bringing home blue ribbons from the American Cheese Society competitions. Don't expect wine with your cheese, though, and you may have to move a bucket of fresh cut flowers off the chair if you need to sit down.

The Garden: The primary appeal of this place to me, a city dweller, is its isolation, the feeling it exudes of independent living, of rejoicing in a clean, healthy environment in which to raise kids, cats, horses, and goats. Don't expect a showplace atmosphere. This is a working farm. Tours are self-guided; although the owners are

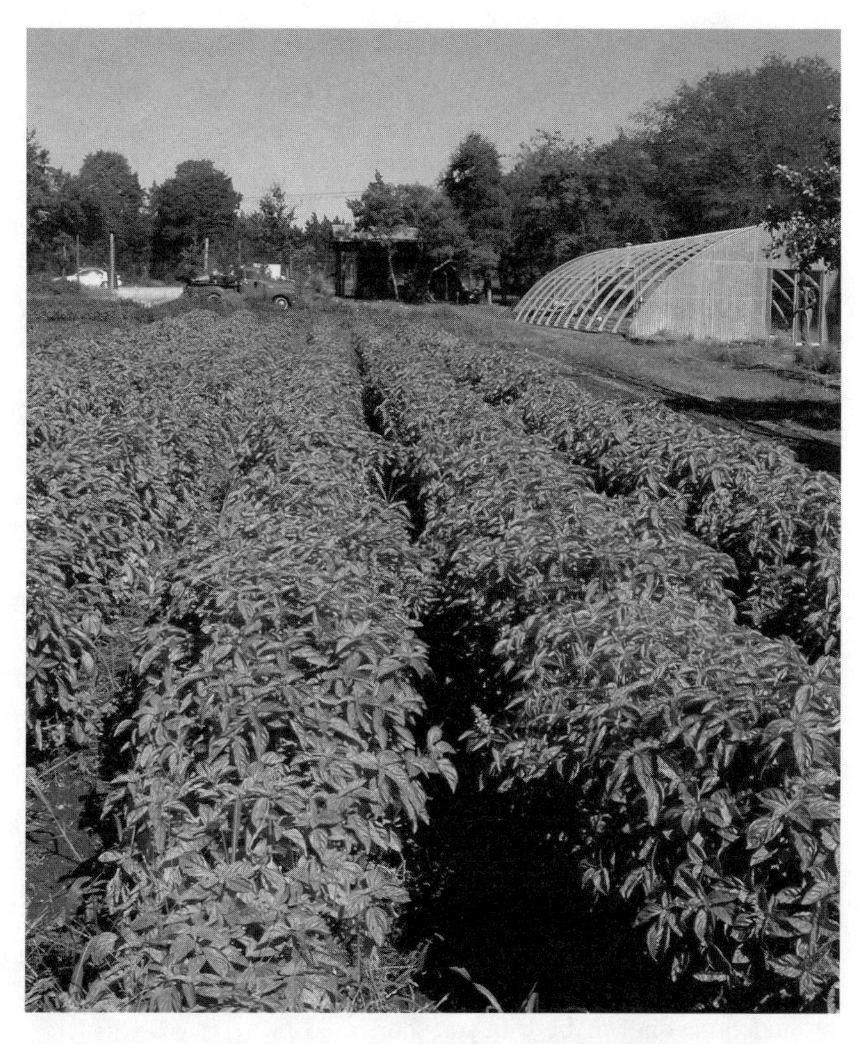

friendly, they're very busy folk, milking goats, making cheese, cutting flowers, and harvesting herbs and baby lettuces for their markets. But they don't mind a bit if you want to wander around the herbs and flowerbeds, admire their handiwork, and select the stems you want to cut. For flowers, choose, according to season, from sunflowers, celosia, gomphrena, zinnia, cosmos, and other hardy beauties. What you don't buy will end up in the hands of the best florists in Austin and San Antonio.

You can buy the farm's products while you're there, if you like, or look for them in Austin and San Antonio at Central Market and Whole Food stores, as well as the Westlake Farmer's Market in Austin, which is open every Saturday throughout the year.

Don't-Miss Feature: Stand quietly for a moment when you first get out of the car and listen to the bird song.

Birds to Watch for: Driving out here, you could come across almost any bird whose habitat is the Edwards Plateau, including golden-cheeked warbler, yellow-billed cuckoo, and wild turkey. Bright-red summer tanager and multi-colored painted bunting are also possible.

Gift Shop: You can buy the farm's products at the stand near the entrance gate.

Tours and Speakers: Although you are welcome to stroll casually among the garden beds when you visit, actual conducted tours of the farm and dairy must be arranged well ahead of time, especially during the busiest spring and fall seasons. Talk to Denny Bolton if you need a knowledgeable speaker for a club or association.

Driving Instructions: On a Saturday, take U.S. Highway 290 about six miles west of Dripping Springs and watch for a small sign on the right that will show you where to turn north. You have some winding around to do on country roads here, so enjoy the birds and wildflowers, but stay alert for signs. When you arrive at the farm, park on the road and walk through the gate. If no one's there, just look around. Someone will be with you shortly.

"What could be more appropriate at a special event than to send wishes of love and goodwill to the heavens on the wings of a butterfly?"

—Deborah Payne, Fredericksburg Butterfly Ranch and Habitat

Fredericksburg

Fredericksburg Butterfly Ranch and Habitat

Fredericksburg
Butterfly Ranch & Habitat
508 W. Main
Fredericksburg, TX 78624
www.livebutterfly.com

508 West Main Street
Fredericksburg, TX 78624
830-990-0735
email: deborah@livebutterfly.com
http://www.livebutterfly.com

Fee: Adults $3; Seniors $2; Children 3-12 $1; under 3 free.

Accessibility: Good.

Days and Hours: The Ranch and Habitat is open March 1 through November 30 from 10-4:30 Tuesday-Saturday, 1-4:30 Sunday. The Butterfly Gift Shop is open 10-5 year round, but closed Sunday through Wednesday from November through February.

Garden Type: Commercial butterfly garden and enclosed habitat, specializing in native butterflies and the plants they depend on.

Garden Size: Fifteen hundred square feet of enclosed habitat, plus space for garden plants.

Themes and Special Features: What do butterflies do all day? You will find out here. Sure, they flitter about, but why? Not only to slurp up nectar from their favorite plants, it seems, but to locate a mate or a sunny basking spot, deposit eggs on the appropriate host plants, sip Gatorade from a human-provided feeder, or puddle about in muddy spots, where they find minerals to supplement their diets. You can see it all here, along with the other forms of the butterfly's life cycle—egg, caterpillar, and chrysalis.

Photo courtesy Fredericksburg Butterfly Ranch

The Gardens: Butterflies not only prefer but sometimes demand specific plants upon which to feed, especially while they are in the caterpillar stage. Monarchs, for instance, depend on milkweed (of which, fortunately, there are some varieties pretty enough for use in the landscape), while Gulf fritillaries demand passion vines, and sulphurs look for clover. Knowing what plants are needed by what butterfly is absolutely key to a working butterfly ranch like this.

How, you might ask, does an enterprise make money raising butterflies? Is there a demand outside the scientific or educational market? Yes, indeed. Butterfly releases, the practice of setting dozens or even hundreds of live butterflies free into the open air, has emerged in the past decade as one of the most romantic rituals available to the celebrant of nuptials or other extraordinary occasions.

Butterflies for release are available in a range of options, from the Individual Release, in which individuals release single butterflies, to the Mass Release, but one of the most satisfying aspects of this business is the way the butterfly wranglers care, and expect their customers to care, for their winged charges. Ranch owner Deborah

Payne has developed special shipping techniques to ensure health and safety during transit, and her detailed instructions make handling and release as non-traumatic an experience for the butterflies as possible. In this way, humans cooperate with nature, rather than exploiting it. The butterflies perform their service of suffusing the ceremony with beauty and then get on with their lives in a new environment.

Don't-Miss Feature: See the stages of metamorphosis in the caterpillar house.

Gift Shop: A special treat awaits butterfly lovers in this little store. Housed in an old home that was built during the town's first year of existence and is now an official Texas Recorded Landmark, it sets the ambience for an adventure in Butterfly Land. Here is everything you always wanted to know about butterflies and didn't know who to ask, along with some of the cutest educational toys you'll find anywhere. Hummingbirds play a role here, too, as do other denizens of the garden. But butterflies are what it's all about. Don't miss it.

Tour Policy: Tours are self-guided, unless you have a large group that needs wrangling. You can set up a guided tour any day except Monday or Thursday for groups of up to 50, but only if you arrange it well in advance. To do so, call 830-990-0735.

Driving Instructions: Main Street (U.S. Highway 290) is right where you would expect to find it in downtown Fredericksburg. The Ranch is on the north side of the street.

Fredericksburg Herb Farm

Bill and Sylvia Varney
402 Whitney Street
Fredericksburg, Texas 78624
830-997-8615; 800-259-4372
email: info@fredericksburgherbfarm.com
http://www.fredericksburgherbfarm.com

 **Fee:** Free.

Accessibility: Generally good throughout. Watch for muddy spots after heavy rains.

Days and Hours: 9:30-5:30 Monday-Saturday; 1-4 Sunday. Closed Christmas, New Year's, Easter, and Thanksgiving Days. Restaurant open for lunch every day. Dinner is served Friday and Saturday evenings only and reservations are required. Call 830-997-8615.

Garden Type: Display herb gardens at retail nursery.

Garden Size: Fourteen acres, including retail.

Themes and Special Features: Five gardens ramble over the property, with the huge Star Garden being the most impressive.

The Gardens: This is a place to immerse yourself in herbs. Literally. You can smell the herbs as you stroll among the numerous gardens, you can eat them in the tiny restaurant, you can have their oils smoothed into your aching muscles in the day spa, or you can buy all of next year's Christmas and birthday presents at once in one of the herb-focused gift shops. Lotions, potions, candles, soaps and oils, vinegars, preserves, spices, ointments, tinctures, and balms. If it's herbal, it's here. As are, of course, the plants themselves.

The farm's owners, Bill and Sylvia Varney, are totally involved in day-to-day operations. They have authored two books about growing and using herbs and developed their own lines of natural herb products. Fourteen acres of gardens produce the herbal underpinnings for all their activities, from aromatherapy offered in the day spa to edible flowers on the restaurant menu. This is basically a working farm and nursery, one that welcomes visitors into the use of herbs in cooking, medicine, cosmetics, decoration, and landscaping.

Organic Maintenance: This is an organically run facility.

Don't-Miss Feature: The lavish lavender in the Star Garden.

Bird Alert: Northern mockingbird is sure to be heard here over the rustic sound of a distant rooster crowing. Colorful house finch or blue grosbeak may come seeking sunflower seeds in the summer. Winter brings an assortment of sparrows, including both white-crowned and white-throated.

Sponsored Activities: An annual Herb Fest in April attracts folks to lectures, demonstrations, tours, and sales featuring herbs and herbal products. Call for current schedule.

Tour Policy: Tours are self-guided. No reservations are necessary. Guided tours are conducted during the annual Herb Fest or by special arrangement. Call the number listed above.

Driving Instructions: From State Highway 290 (Main Street), follow Milam Street south about half a mile until it dead ends. Look to your right. You'll see the Herb Farm.

"Rub thy face with violets and goat's milk, and there is not a prince in the world who will not follow thee."

Old Gaelic beauty tip quoted by Bill and Sylvia Varney in *Herbs: Growing and Using the Plants of Romance*

The Japanese Garden of Peace

The National Museum of the Pacific War
340 East Main Street
Fredericksburg, Texas 78624
830-997-4379
http://www.tpwd.state.tx.us/park/nimitz

Fee: Adult $5; Student with I.D. $3; Children under 6 free; Members free.

Accessibility: Excellent.

Days and Hours: 10:00-5:00 every day of the year except Christmas.

Garden Type: Traditional Japanese garden, elegant in its simplicity.

Garden Size: Very small.

Themes and Special Features: Sited in the courtyard of a museum complex, this garden serves as a symbol of post-World War II friendship and reconciliation. It was built by Japanese craftsmen as a gift from the military leaders of Japan to the people of the United States, in honor of Fleet Admiral Chester W. Nimitz. Its design, a replica of the garden owned by Admiral Togo in Japan, emphasizes the classical elements of stone, raked gravel, plants, and water, used to symbolize the balance of nature. It also contains a traditional structure called a meditation study, a duplicate of Admiral Togo's.

Sponsored Activities: The museum that houses the Peace Garden is dedicated to the action that took place in the Pacific Theater during World War II. You don't have to be a war-history buff to find the exhibits fascinating, especially the aircraft, tanks, and guns used by both the Allies and the Japanese and the mockups of famous events, like Doolittle preparing to raid Tokyo.

ADMIT ONE **Tour Policy:** Tours of the garden are self-guided. Groups of 20 or more are eligible for a reduced admission if reservations are made ahead. Call 830-997-4379.

Volunteer and Support Opportunities: Like most museums, this one can always use volunteers. Call about opportunities to work in the garden itself.

Driving Instructions: Main Street runs east and west through the heart of Fredericksburg. You won't have any trouble locating the museum.

Wildseed Farms

WILDSEED FARMS

425 Wildflower Hills
P.O. Box 3000
Fredericksburg, Texas 78624
830-990-1393; 800-848-0078
email: wsf@fbg.net
http://www.wildseedfarms.com

Fee: Free.

Accessibility: Excellent in the display garden and shopping areas.

Days and Hours: 9:30-5:00 in winter, until 6 in summer.

Garden Type: This is both a working farm, a world leader in producing wildflower seed, and a fantastic display garden set up to give visitors a close-up view of the some of the crops.

Garden Size: Two hundred acres in production at this site, including 70 acres of bluebonnets. Trails through the growing areas and beside sizeable display beds.

Themes and Special Features: It's all about flowers here—both native and introduced species that have proven themselves adaptable to wild-like growing conditions. This company sells flower seeds by mail to folks all over the world. It's the largest working farm in the nation that grows wildflower seeds and sells them directly to the customer. The chance to tour their growing operation is a treat.

The Pick-Your-Own-Bouquet field lets you cut your own flowers at a very reasonable price. Buy a container in the gift shop. Shears are furnished.

The Gardens: Timing your visit is key here. Although there will be something in bloom from early spring until frost, March through May and September through November are prime times for the most spectacular shows. In the spring, look for bluebonnet, of course, including the famous maroon one recently introduced to the market, but also red corn poppy, California poppy, larkspur, and bachelor button. These later give way to zinnia, petunia, cosmos, and other summer bloomers. In late fall, yellow sunflowers, blue and purple salvias, and white daisies keep up the show.

Don't-Miss Feature: Plan to spend some time in the gift shop, which they call the Market Center, where you will find not only flower seeds for sale but also everything Texas-y, from T-shirts to teacups. If ice cream, beer, or a snack appeals to you, head through the store to the Brew-Bonnet Bier Garten refreshment area. You can see lots of flower fields from there and enjoy a cool one at the same time.

Bird Alert: Look for greater roadrunner sprinting along a row of wildflowers. Hawks soaring overhead may be Cooper's or red-shouldered.

Tour Policy: Tours are self-guided. No reservations are necessary.

Driving Instructions: The farm is located on State Highway 290 about seven miles east of Fredericksburg. Watch for it on the south side of the road. It's the beautiful cedar log "horse barn" sitting amidst acres of rows of flowers.

Why Some Bluebonnets Are Pink

Bluebonnets actually occur in a range of colors, including the maroon developed at Wildseed Farms in Fredericksburg. Greg Grant of Stephen F. Austin University in Nacogdoches tells a charming story about how some—only a very few—bluebonnets became pink.

There have always been white ones, he says, mixed in with the blue, but pink ones occur naturally only in San Antonio, along a road within sight of the Alamo. Legend has it that they arose after the famous battle fought there, colored by the blood of heroes that spilled over the land.

Georgetown

City of Poppies

Georgetown Convention & Visitors Bureau
P.O. Box 409
Georgetown, Texas 78627-0409
512-930-3545; 800-436-8696
email: tmorris@georgetowntx.org
http://www.georgetown.org

Fee: Free.

Accessibility: This is mostly a driving tour.

Days and Hours: Daylight hours in March and April.

Garden Type: The whole city of Georgetown turns into a garden in early spring, decorated by the poppies that turn the landscape scarlet, just as they've been doing for over 70 years. They come from naturalized plantings that reseed each year. The original seeds were sent home from the European front after World War I by Henry Purl Compton. His mother planted them at 507 E. 7th Street, and they have spread from there. These are the variety of poppies made famous by John McCrea's poem, "In Flanders fields the poppies blow, Between the crosses, row on row. . . ."

Poppies won't be the only things blooming at this time of year, of course. Bluebonnets, paintbrushes, blanketflower, and evening primrose should be putting on a show, as well.

Garden Size: Most of the old town and along the river.

Themes and Special Features: Of course, the good people of this Great American Main Street community wouldn't miss the chance to celebrate their famous bloomers with a "Red Poppy Festival" in early April, a street fair that includes a parade, food vendors, arts and crafts displays, and lots of music. Call the Main Street Manager at 800-436-8696 to get the exact date.

Driving Instructions: Georgetown lies about 26 miles north of Austin on IH-35. It's sometimes called "the Gateway to the Hill Country."

Harwood

Kactus Korral

7715 U.S. Highway 90 West
Harwood, Texas 78632-4747
830-540-3568
email: kactus@kactus.com
http://www.kactuskorral.com

Fee: Free.

Accessibility: Excellent.

Days and Hours: Normal business hours.

Garden Type: Not really a garden at all, this retail nursery, located literally in the middle of nowhere, is simply not to be missed if you're in the vicinity. It sells nothing but cacti and other succulents.

Garden Size: One huge greenhouse is open to the public. Over fifty others are devoted to the production of plants for the wholesale industry.

Themes and Special Features: Cactus, cactus, cactus. And other succulents, too. An RV park is located next to the retail store.

The Gardens: Hundreds of varieties in thousands and thousands of pots, dish gardens, hanging baskets, and planters, ranging in size from two inches to too big to transport in the average automobile. When this place is in bloom, and it always seems to be, the effect is of a confetti factory exploding with neon colors—yellow, orange, pink, and red. Even not in bloom, the plants offer enough variety of size, color, and visual texture to make a visit worthwhile. I am, myself, not a cactus lover, but when I see the variety and beauty laid out here, even I can see why they are so collectible.

Don't-Miss Feature: Rest a moment in the shade of the huge old oak in front of the retail store. Gives you a new appreciation for trees on a hot day.

Bird Alert: Look up. You're sure to see a hawk or two circling overhead. Could be red-tailed, red-shouldered, northern harrier, sharp-shinned, or Cooper's. Or, on the other hand, could be a black or turkey vulture. Take your binoculars.

Tour Policy: Tour buses are always welcome.

Gift Shop: There's not a large selection in the little convenience store, but you can get a bottle of water if looking at all that cactus has made you thirsty, as well as helpful information about choosing plants and caring for them.

Driving Instructions: From IH-10, between Houston and San Antonio, take Exit 642 and go north about two miles to the intersection of U.S. Highway 90 and State Highway 304. Look left. You can't miss it. There's nothing else out there.

Independence

The Antique Rose Emporium

10000 Highway 50
Brenham, Texas 77833
(see Driving Instructions below)
979-836-5548
email: roses@industryinet.com
http://www.antiqueroseemporium.com or www.weareroses.com

Fee: Free.

Accessibility: Good. Some stone paths can be a bit rough; there's a good scattering of nicely shaded benches about the property.

Days and Hours: 9-6 Monday-Saturday; 11-5:30 Sunday.

Garden Type: Display garden at retail and mail order nursery.

Garden Size: Five acres.

Themes and Special Features: Rose Garden, Cottage Garden, Herb Garden, Children's Garden, Butterfly Garden, Water Gardens, and more.

The Garden: This is my very favorite garden in the entire state of Texas. And it's not just me. Set among gentle swells in the valley of the Brazos River, this retail nursery and display garden has become a first-class attraction for gardeners and rose lovers from across the southern United States. Offering over 400 varieties of old-fashioned roses, displayed amidst a five-acre cottage garden, the Emporium provides an experience that will bring you slogging back over the prairie again and again, as it has me.

Across that very same prairie in covered wagons is how many of the featured roses first entered Texas, to be planted by settlers in cottage gardens and cemeteries and left, often untended, to make their own way in the vicissitudes of the Texas climate. Talk about tough! (And you thought roses were sissies.) Cuttings passed from hand to hand over a century and a half filled the South with such proven survivors at the same time the nursery industry lost interest in the older rose forms and poured all its resources into developing and marketing hybrid teas. Those are the long-stemmed, usually odorless, disease-and-pest-prone delicate darlings that have since given roses their reputation as being hard for the homeowner to grow.

In the 1980s Michael Shoup and Bill Welch began to rediscover this treasure stash of old jewels along roadsides, at abandoned farmhouses, and in neglected cemeteries. Tutored by their friend Pam Puryear, who'd been doing it for years, they began to take cuttings, and soon they were raising old roses for commerce. Today Shoup owns the Antique Rose Emporium.

Its five acres showcase restored 19th-century buildings, including a stone kitchen built in 1855 and surviving from the original home that stood on this site, a salt-box house, an old log corn crib, a Victorian home, and a wedding chapel, all set amidst a glory of climbing, running, shimmering, glorious roses, both in beds for display and in pots for sale. You're asked not to pick the blooms, of course, but indulge yourself in sniffing.

Since most of these roses resist pests and disease on their own, they don't require much spraying, so the smell of chemical sprays won't interfere with your pleasure the way they do in some rose gardens. Just make sure a blossom doesn't harbor a wee happy bee before you stick your nose in it.

But roses are not the only allure here. The Herb Garden, its entrance flanked by sweet bay trees underplanted with garlic chives, is one of the best expositions of herb use in the landscape you will find anywhere. Rosemaries, mint marigolds, and seasonal vegetables join perennials, small shrubs, and roses in a display of cottage gardening at its most exuberant.

Don't-Miss Features: It would take most of a long summer day to explore and fully appreciate the nooks, whimsies, and secret gardens scattered throughout the grounds. The longer you stroll about, the more wonders you will discover, first among them the pervading sense of whimsy that expresses itself in home-made garden art, old garden implements, such as rusty barrows planted with colorful annuals, and most saliently in the Children's Garden just inside the west gate, the Beatrix Potter Garden. Here, past the McGregor Farm mailbox, you will find charming beds of vegetables and flowers labeled with handmade signs, marking "Tiggywinkle Well" and "Puddleduck Pond." The gardeners here are child-sized figures made of little terra-cotta pots stacked together in clever shapes—one climbing a tree, one fishing in a minuscule pond, one "pedaling" an ancient tricycle, with succulents and sedums sprouting from its head and joints. This tiny garden alone is worth coming here to see.

Once you leave the children's garden, be sure to check out the bottle tree, also near the west gate. Green, brown, gold, and clear bottles seem to sprout from a dead tree, the embodiment of an ancient superstition about trapping evil spirits and imprisoning them in glass bottles. (I remember similar sights from my childhood in West Texas, but most of them seemed to favor the cobalt blue once so popular in chemist's and beverage bottles.)

And then there's the concrete alligator lurking below a bridge as you make your way through the water features. Kids will love it.

Birds to Watch for: On these rolling prairies, birds abound. Red-tailed and red-shouldered hawks will be soaring overhead. Look for ruby-throated hummingbirds among the flowers.

Sponsored Activities: Educating the public about the virtues of old roses is a passion for the folks who work here. A three-day Fall Festival of Roses held in November brings rosarians and other plant experts in for seminars and workshops geared to the public. The nursery also publishes a 100-page, full-color catalog for their mail order business that is so informative it can serve as the basis for an education in old roses. There is a charge for the catalog, so have your credit card ready if you want to order one before you go. Call 800-441-0002. They also offer a smaller free catalog, or you can check out rose selections on their web site.

Tour and Rental Policies: No more delightful place can be imagined for a group tour, but you are requested to call ahead to make arrangements, so a staff member can be available to help you corral your garden enthusiasts and make the most of the visit.

If you're picturing a wedding or reception held under giant Montezuma cypress trees, with a backdrop of roses and herbs, call 409-836-5548. They'll provide the information you need and help you make arrangements.

Gift Shop: You will stumble across more than one gift shop display, but the main store is Trellises and Treasures, featuring, as you might imagine, rose-themed gifts, but also more practical items such as seeds, bulbs, tools, and books. The Stone Kitchen Garden Shop is housed in the 1855 kitchen building.

Mail Order: If you see a rose that you absolutely must have for your very own, you don't have to buy it while you're here and baby it through a car trip back home. In fact, the bulk of this company's business is mail order. Pick up a catalog, or see their web site at www.weareroses.com to order whatever strikes your fancy. All roses are grown on their own roots and shipped in two-gallon containers from October through April every year.

Driving Instructions: The Antique Rose Emporium lies between Austin and Houston and between Brenham and Bryan-College Station on State Highway 50, just south of the minute town of Independence. Get out your state highway map. You're going to need it.

Wildflower Alert: If you are in this area any time from late March through April, consult your map again to find the best country roads for wildflower viewing. Check out Farm Roads 390, 50, 912, and 1155 in the vicinity of Brenham.

Heritage Roses: A Treasure Lost and Found

Like any other human enterprise with a commercial component, flowers are subject to the vagaries of fashion, and none more so than the rose. Until the mid-eighteenth century, no one in Europe or America had heard of a rose that bloomed much more than once a year, and usually in the spring for only a few weeks.

When, in the 1700s, intrepid businessmen began opening the Orient to trade with the West, one of the first things to emerge from China was a type of rose that bloomed repeatedly throughout the growing season. Rose growers and breeders in Europe and America went wild, crossing the roses they knew with these foreign cousins. Within a hundred years, they had developed literally thousands of new rose varieties and introduced them to the buying public.

Old Blush, the first China rose to arrive in Europe, later came into Texas with the first pioneers, as did thousands of her sisters as potted plants or rooted cuttings (it's said that some traveled rooted in potatoes) and made themselves at home beside rough log cabins on newly cleared sites all across the state. Soon their names, many of them hard to pronounce and impossible to spell or simply not considered important, faded from memory and were replaced by sensible, meaningful names. Souvenir de la Malmaison, for instance, introduced at the French court in 1843, might be known as Aunt Polly in one pioneer settlement and as Duncan's Rose in another, named for the person who first grew the rose in a neighborhood or who gave all his friends and relatives cuttings. Original names were lost.

Since roses are relatively easy to propagate, even for amateurs, early Texans planted them everywhere, including places where no one would be around to water, feed, prune, or otherwise care for them, like cemeteries. Some, it turned out, couldn't adapt to the cold in parts of Texas. Others succumbed to fungal diseases, died of thirst, or drowned. But many survived, not only untended in old cemeteries, but on the sites of abandoned farmhouses, city gardens, and Aunt Polly's or Duncan's backyard, and in the gardens of all their nephews and cousins.

Meanwhile, fashion passed them by. By the turn of the twentieth century, a hundred and fifty years after the first Asian rose entered Europe, one hybrid class dominated the market. The hybrid tea rose had captured the hearts of the public, at least in America. With her huge, classically shaped blooms in almost every bright color imaginable and stiff, leggy stems for cutting, she was the dream flower. Soon, retail nurseries carried little else, and when Americans planted roses, they planted hybrid teas. Today, when you say "rose," the picture you invoke in most folks' minds is of a hybrid tea like Peace or Tropicana.

But in much of the American South, including Texas, this worldly beauty soon displayed a lack of character. She was prone to disease in our humid summers, for instance, or tended to faint in the heat, or it turned out that her high breeding had left something out—fragrance.

So, while a few varieties proved themselves stalwarts under local conditions, Oklahoma, for instance, comes to mind and Mr. Lincoln, and Peace, Crimson Glory, and Double Delight, most others did not. Roses gained a reputation for being fussy and hard to grow in many parts of Texas. A whole industry grew up to develop and sell pungent chemicals to feed and medicate them.

When you entered a rose garden, it didn't matter that many of the roses had no fragrance. You wouldn't have been able to enjoy it, anyway, because of the cloud of noxious chemicals hanging in the air. So I grew up thinking that roses were nice when you worked at them, but not worth the trouble for a basically laissez-faire gardener like me, who had no truck whatsoever with synthetic fertilizers and fungicides.

Then in the 1980s I began to hear about a kind of rose that was new on the market in Texas but that, confusingly enough, was called "old." Some of the better nurseries in Dallas and San Antonio were selling it. That was the beginning of another revolution in rose fashion for our part of the world. The old pioneer roses had been rediscovered.

Suddenly, Souvenir de la Malmaison appeared at my neighborhood nursery, its name rediscovered and reattached. There was Old Blush, too, Cecile Brunner and Duchesse de Brabant and Ducher, and what some claim is the original "yellow rose of Texas," Fortune's Double Yellow. Where were they coming from? From the very cemeteries and dooryards and cottage gardens where they and their descendants had been living untended for a hundred years—unpruned, unwatered, unfertilized.

Historians, rosarians, and business people had joined hands to re-introduce many older roses to the gardening public. The market fairly exploded. People like me began to demand more choice. We wanted access to bourbons and noisettes and Chinas and teas, and to more modern classes like floribunda and miniature and shrub. And we got it. I made the plunge into heritage roses in my garden and never looked back.

Today almost thirty old roses make their homes in my backyard, and you will find heirloom specimens forming the backbone of many a public garden all over the state. Whether you call them "old," "antique," "heritage," or "heirloom," we're proud of our pioneer roses.

My Favorite Old Roses

My favorite old roses are those that are profligate in their blooms, never need pruning, never get sick, and ask for food only once or twice a year. I don't mind watering them. We all need some extra hydration during July and August in Texas.

First on my list is "Caldwell Pink," probably a Polyantha, which was found growing near Caldwell, Texas, and brought to market under this study name. It blooms continuously in my garden from early May until a hard freeze toward the end of November. Small, lavender-pink, multi-petal blossoms cover the shrub, which is about four feet tall and wide, and brighten the landscape like nothing else. It comes in a climbing version, too.

Blooming almost as frequently but more mannerly in the number of blossoms is Duchesse de Brabant, a pink tea introduced to the market over a hundred and fifty years ago, and still one of the most fragrant roses ever bred. As with all my favorites, the foliage is totally disease free in my humid northeast Texas landscape. I usually prune this rose lightly during late winter.

The white rose in my garden is a China called "Ducher." Known to the market since 1869, this handsome, healthy shrub just can't seem to stop blooming and spreading its sweet, fruity fragrance around the garden. The petals drop cleanly, and new growth is a vibrant maroon, so the plant looks good all season.

Louis Phillippe or Cramoisi Superieur provides a constant fragrant bloom of such a deep rose-pink as to be called "red" in the parlance of old roses. The two Chinas are so similar that some experts think they may be the same rose, but in any case, both are tough, long-blooming, and gorgeous, a staple in many southern gardens.

Kerrville

Riverside Nature Center

150 Francisco Lemos Street
P.O. Box 645
Kerrville, Texas 78029
830-257-4837
email: mca@ktc.com
http://www.ktc.net/riverside

 **Fee:** Free.

Accessibility: Good.

 **Days and Hours:** Trail open daily during daylight hours. The office is open 9-4 Monday-Friday, 10-2 Saturday.

Garden Type: Nature center and trail featuring native plants and wildlife.

Garden Size: Five acres.

Themes and Special Features: This is a Certified Wildscape Demonstration Center.

The Gardens: Where the Guadalupe River and Town Creek come together, you will find an unusually welcoming Visitor Center and a well-marked botanical garden featuring more than 100 native tree species and some 200 species of wildflowers and grasses. A Xeric Garden shows off cacti and succulents, and birds, lizards, butterflies, and other wildlife make themselves at home.

Don't-Miss Feature: Take the walking trail down to the banks of the river. Look for the Butterfly Garden. Appreciate the cypress trees.

Bird Alert: Four rare or endangered species may be encountered in Kerr County: golden-cheeked warbler, black-capped vireo, green kingfisher, and zone-tailed hawk. Red-shouldered hawk is resident here. This is a great place for spring warblers, especially along the creek.

Sponsored Activities: The Center often sponsors talks, lectures, and other events, including a spring home and garden tour. Call for the latest schedule.

Tour Policy: Tours are self-guided.

Gift Shop: A small shop is open six days a week in the Visitor Center, where you will find books and nature-related gifts and crafts.

Volunteer and Support Opportunities: The Riverside Nature Center Association is the philanthropic organization that helps support the Center. They will welcome your contributions or volunteer efforts. You can reach them at the number above.

Driving Instructions: Take Farm Road 27 north from downtown Kerrville. Drive about half a dozen blocks and turn left on Francisco Lemos Street. Look for the sign on your left.

Lampasas

Hickory Hill Herbs and Antique Roses

307 West Avenue E
Lampasas, Texas 76550
512-556-8801
email: hillherb@dashlink.com
http://www.hickoryhillherbs.com

Fee: Free.

Accessibility: Limited.

Days and Hours: Open 9-5 Monday-Saturday; other times by appointment.

Garden Type: Small display garden at retail nursery.

Garden Size: Backyard sized.

Themes and Special Features: A cottage garden certified as a Texas Wildscape, this display features old roses, herbs, and native plants, along with a "taste and scent tour" of the place. The gardens are intended to educate customers on the landscaping and gardening potential in herbs and old roses, native perennials, and butter-fly-attracting plants.

Gift Shop: Look here for topiaries, herbal soaps and lotions, gifts, and garden products.

Bird Alert: Carolina chickadee and Bewick's wren like these environs.

Sponsored Activities: Owners Don and Paula Hill participate in the annual Herb and Art Fest the second Saturday of each October in Lampasas. A good part of what they do here at the nursery involves teaching others to be comfortable with herbs and roses.

Tour Policy: Tours are self-guided. Or Don or Paula can show you around.

Driving Instructions: U.S. Highway 183/281 runs north and south through Lampasas. You'll turn west onto West Avenue E on the far north side of town.

Round Top

The City of Round Top

Round Top Chamber of Commerce
North Washington Street
Round Top, Texas 78954
979-249-4042
email: roundtop@cvtv.net
http://www.roundtop.com

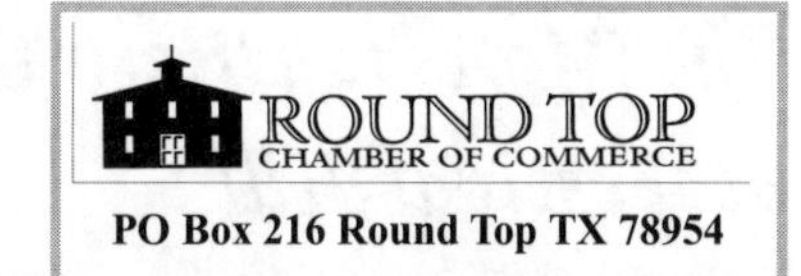

This is the heart of wildflower country, so during spring and fall you may have trouble looking at anything else, but the tiny hamlet of Round Top is worth slowing down for almost anytime of the year. Located on Highway 237 between LaGrange and Brenham, it's home to bed and breakfasts in beautifully restored historic houses, first-rate art galleries, craft shops, and antique and gift shops.

The special activities hosted here, from antique and trades shows to Shakespeare performances and classical-music concerts, go on year round and are too numerous to list. The Chamber of Commerce will be glad to provide you with a current schedule of events. You can tour a dairy farm here or an old car museum, hike a nature trail, or explore an herb garden. And that brings us to the subject at hand.

Many of the homes and B and Bs, as well as some other businesses, maintain lovely flower and herb gardens. They will not want you tromping through them, but make the block and gawk a bit from your car. Other properties are open to the public. One place where you can stroll around is the herb garden located on the grounds of **Landhaus Ramsey Restaurant and Biergarten**, on Highway 237 (Washington Street), about three blocks south of the downtown square. A 275-year-old live oak tree dominates the property, while roses and other perennials set off the wooden structures, one of which is a hand-hewn double log cabin. The restaurant's hours vary, so call if you want to have dinner, 979-249-2080.

At the historic restoration project called Henkel Square just east of the town square, a faithfully restored 19th-century village includes an herb garden and a kitchen garden, as well as specimens of the old roses early settlers would have brought with them to plant in this area.

The McAshan Herb Gardens at Festival Hill

Attention: Gwen Barclay
P.O. Box 89
Round Top, Texas 78954-0089 (see Driving Instructions below)
979-249-5283
email: gwenbarclay_herbs@hotmail.com
http://www.festivalhill.org

Fee: None to walk the grounds. Guided tours can be arranged for a fee, or you can participate in one of the Herb Days at Festival Hill described below.

Accessibility: Very variable, poor to good.

Days and Hours: You can walk around the gardens whenever you wish during daylight hours.

Garden Type: Herb gardens, cottage gardens.

The Gardens: The International Festival-Institute at Round Top is a two-hundred-acre campus for the advanced training of

gifted young professional musicians. It is also the venue for concerts, recitals, lectures, seminars, and business retreats. Several historic structures are found here housing examples of Texas carpentry, as well as furnishings and collections reflecting varied interests. The herb gardens found on the grounds are some of the largest in the state.

Built on several levels in a rather wild setting near the banks of a lake, it thrives under the care of Madalene Hill and Gwen Barclay, co-authors of one of my favorite books, *Southern Herb Growing*. Here, the mother and daughter team conduct tours and seminars in spring and fall each year. Enrollment in these very popular events is necessarily limited, so make your reservations well ahead.

The first of these, "Herb Days at Festival Hill," is held in spring and fall. Each day includes a guided tour of the herb gardens, a three-course luncheon prepared with fresh herbs, and an educational lecture. The cost is about $30.

For those who want to know more, the herbal seminars provide in-depth educational opportunities and include a light luncheon buffet, printed materials, and tastings or take-homes from the workshops. Topics vary, ranging from "Making Herbal Liqueurs" or "Herbal Vinaigrettes" to "Growing, Harvesting and Using Culinary Herbs." The cost is about $50. For about $60, there's the Annual Herbal Forum at Round Top, with a full day's activities, including plant sales, luncheon and tea, and workshops conducted by experts.

Don't-Miss Feature: The stone work you encounter here that looks so much like Roman ruins is the work of artist Jack Finke. It seems designed to emphasize the Mediterranean spirit that runs through the herb garden. If you take the gravel drive down into the property, don't miss his two old-looking stone bridges at the west end. But don't spend too much time trying to figure out what all these massive artworks represent. Their purpose is thematic rather than representational. Just enjoy their picturesque and unique contribution to the ambience of Festival Hill.

Themes and Special Features: You'll find lavender in raised beds, huge rosemaries, and a pharmaceutical garden on the east side of the house. At least 80 varieties of rosemary and 20 of lavender are being grown here, as is a Fruit Tree Garden featuring pomegranates, rare figs, jujube, and citrus. In the shaded areas, ginseng and cohosh grow, as do exotic black pepper and other spices. Stone paths lead you on a ramble through a series of informal plantings of herbs and perennials on the west side. A graveled drive leads down to a more formal garden on the north. This is the most accessible area.

Near the greenhouse you'll find the Pharmacy Garden, raised beds filled with medicinal plants from India, Asia, South America, and around the world.

Bird Alert: If you come here on a weekday or during the winter, you'll often find yourself the only visitor. Step quietly, and the birds may not even notice you're there. Expect to see blue jay, of course, along with Carolina chickadee, eastern bluebird, tufted titmouse, and if you're very lucky, painted bunting. Woodpeckers include red-headed and downy, and you might just spot a curve-billed thrasher thrashing about among the fallen leaves.

Tour Policy: Tours of the McAshan Gardens or Festival Hill grounds can be arranged by calling 979-249-3129.

Driving Instructions: On the north side of town, turn west off Highway 237 (Washington Street) onto Jaster Road, the entrance to the grounds of Festival Hill. Look for signs to the parking lot. This is the home of the International Festival-Institute. McAshan Gardens lie on the north side of the road (on your right as you enter) around the Menke House. Look for the sign.

San Antonio

Japanese Tea Garden (Chinese Tea Garden, Sunken Garden)

3853 N. St. Mary's Street
San Antonio, Texas 78212
210-207-3000

 **Fee:** Free.

Accessibility: Although this garden was built in 1918 in a highly inaccessible location, studded with rough paths, curving staircases, and stone bridges, today, thanks to the efforts of the city's Parks and Recreation Department, accessibility is excellent. If the tiny parking lot in front of the garden is full, you'll find more parking at the entrance to the Sunken Garden Theater next door. Both lots provide good access to the grounds.

 **Days and Hours:** 8:30 A.M. to 10:00 P.M., closing at 5:00 P.M. on Memorial Day and Labor Day.

Garden Type: Japanese-style garden, with large lily pond and lush semitropical plantings. Contains many more flowering plants than most gardens of this type, incorporating native perennials and colorful annuals throughout.

Garden Recognition: This site is designated as a Texas Civil Engineering Landmark and a Registered Texas Historic Landmark and is listed on the National Register of Historic Places.

Themes and Special Features: A sunken garden with an oriental theme, built on several levels within an old stone quarry between 1917 and 1918. Don't miss the path across a bridge that leads up to the old kiln tower. White stone buildings at the base of the tower lend an enchanted air to the entryway. The city built them in 1920 to house the making and sale of Mexican arts and crafts. Disused today, they still display a charm that sets the scene for the very unusual garden that lies behind them.

The Garden: Unique, breathtaking, historic, intriguing—how to describe this miniature jewel hidden in San Antonio's huge Brackenridge Park? It is all that and more. The old quarry in which it sits acts not only as a supporting structure for the garden, but also as a thematic element, as stone upon stone beside stone defines paths, walls, bridges, and the pagoda that dominates the whole. Plantings are lush to the point of extravagance, with emphasis more on color and texture than on maintaining a real oriental feel in the material. An astounding variety of flora lines the curving stone walkways around the lily pond at the garden's center, all healthy-looking and well cared for. Huge old trees lend shade, while gracefully shaped stone stairs proclaim the oriental theme.

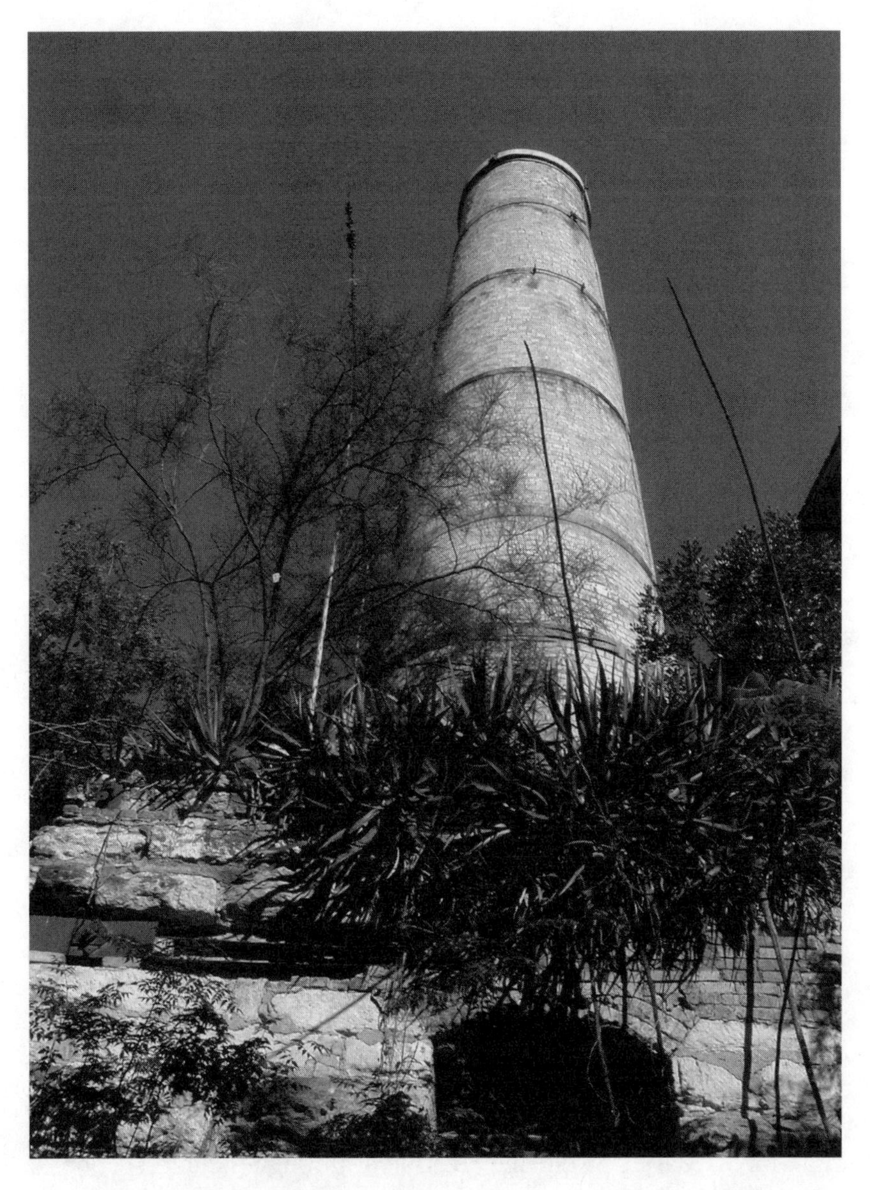

Any successful garden spirits the visitor out of the ordinary and into a world of its own creation. This little space, so self-contained and replete with beauties, draws the visitor into its world with no fanfare. A discreet bronze marker explains how the garden, designed and built by a city parks commissioner and a local Japanese-American artist during World War I, was renamed the Chinese Sunken Garden upon the outbreak of World War II. Kimi Eizo Jingu, who not only had helped bring the garden into being but had lived there with his family for two decades, was evicted. It was not until 1984 that Jingu's descendants saw the rededication of the garden as the Japanese Tea Garden, with proper recognition paid to their talented ancestor.

If you are fond of Japanese gardens, make a point of visiting the Kumamoto En in the San Antonio Botanical Gardens, as well as this one. The contrast between the exuberance of the Sunken Garden and the restraint of the Kumamoto, both effective designs, will stretch your concepts of style and enrich your appreciation of both.

Don't-Miss Feature: Watch for the turtles sunning themselves on exposed surfaces in the pond.

Bird Alert: This is a very popular garden within a confined space. When visitor activity is high, bird activity probably won't be. But stay alert. The hummingbird you'll encounter here in the summer will most likely be the black-chinned hummingbird. You may also glimpse a golden-fronted woodpecker, a Carolina wren, or house finch, none of which are known for their shyness. In winter, when things quiet down, look for yellow-bellied sapsucker, rufous-sided towhee, and sparrows such as white-throated, Lincoln's, song, and fox sparrows.

Tour and Rental Policy: This garden seems tailor made for weddings, receptions, and other romantic to-dos. Check with Parks and Recreation at 210-207-7275.

Driving Instructions: From downtown San Antonio, take State Highway 281 north to the St. Mary's Street exit. Turn right on St. Mary's Street and go straight through the intersection. If you see signs directing you toward the zoo, you're on the right track. You will find the garden on your left, about half a mile past the intersection.

King William Historical District

Fee: Free, except as shown below.

Accessibility: Varies; much can be seen from a car.

Days and Hours: Daylight hours.

Garden Type: The King William Historic District is a 25-block area of private homes, only two of which are regularly open to the public. They are the Edward Steves Homestead and the Guenther House. Of the other houses and gardens, including several bed and breakfast establishments, you are welcome to look at what you can see from the car or by strolling by, but treat these properties as private homes.

Garden Size: Varies.

Themes and Special Features: Springtime brings the colors to life in this lovely old district, but it's a rewarding sight anytime of the year, with its ancient towering trees, dense evergreens, and almost ever-blooming roses.

The Gardens: The Edward Steves Homestead is located at 509 King William. The house and gardens are maintained as an historic museum and are open to the public from 10-4 daily. Adult admission to the home is $3. Children under 12 are free. The phone number is 210-227-9160.

The Guenther House at 205 E. Guenther is the original home of Pioneer Flour Mills founder Carl Guenther. It houses a museum featuring flour mill memorabilia and a collection of Dresden china. There's a store selling gourmet food items and an excellent restaurant here, too. The museum and store are open 9-5 Monday through Saturday and 8-2 Sunday. The restaurant serves from 7-3 Monday through Saturday and 8-2 Sunday. The phone number is 210-227-1061.

Driving Instructions: The district lies on the south bank of the San Antonio River near downtown. Take Saint Mary's

Street south, past Durango, and then turn right on King William. Or walk down the Riverwalk from downtown to Durango Street.

Marion Koogler McNay Art Museum

6000 New Braunfels
San Antonio, Texas 78209
210-824-5368
http://www.mcnayart.org

TheMcNay
The Marion Koogler McNay Art Museum

Fee: Free except during some special events.

Accessibility: Wheelchairs are available. Accessibility varies outdoors, but is excellent in the museum.

Days and Hours: The grounds are open from 7 A.M. until 7 P.M. from April through October, closing at 6 P.M. November through March. The Museum is open 10-5 Tuesday-Saturday; 12-5 Sunday. Closed Monday, July 4, and Thanksgiving, Christmas, and New Year's Days.

Garden Type: Estate garden at what was once a private home, now a major-collections art museum home to many masterpieces of 19th- and 20th-century art.

Garden Size: The estate covers 23 acres.

Themes and Special Features: A courtyard sculpture garden and a Japanese-style garden. Towering old trees lend a majestic touch.

The Gardens: If you enjoy serious art, you will love this place. As quiet, restrained, and tastefully appointed as the museum itself, the grounds lack the showy boisterousness of some gardens, relying on the lure of shaded paths and carefully selected artwork for their appeal. Trees star in this landscape, with color only where and when appropriate.

Don't-Miss Feature: The gazebo and pond area are exquisite.

Bird Alert: City birds abound here. Listen for mourning dove.

Sponsored Activities: Activities here center around the museum and its exhibits, but something is always going on. Their education department serves more than 40,000 people a year. Pick up a current schedule of events.

Tour Policy: Tours, lectures, and performances are ongoing for the museum itself. At 3:15 the first Sunday of the month, docents give a tour featuring the highlights of the museum. Tours of the grounds are strictly self-guided.

Gift Shop: The Museum Store located on the first floor of the museum stocks a very impressive array of art-related items, including books and gifts. The store's phone number is 210-805-1732.

Volunteer and Support Opportunities: The McNay was the first museum of modern art in Texas. If you would like to help support it, you will find a range of memberships available, all with excellent member benefits. 210-805-1756.

Driving Instructions: North New Braunfels runs parallel with and to the east of U.S. Highway 281. You can exit U.S. 281 North at Hildebrand Avenue and go east. At Broadway, turn north (left). In less than a mile, you will be veering east (right) onto Austin Highway. When Austin Highway intersects with North New Braunfels, turn north (left). Two or three hundred feet down the road there will be a gated driveway on the right. Watch for the sign.

From IH-410, the exit to take is Nacogdoches Road South. Drive south to the intersection of Nacogdoches with North New Braunfels and turn left. A little more than a mile down the road, you will pass a shopping center on the left. Look for the gated entryway just past it.

Paseo del Rio/Riverwalk

San Antonio Parks and Recreation
454 Soledad, River Suite #2
San Antonio, Texas 78205
210-207-7275

Fee: Free.

Accessibility: Varies; accessible from some locations. Call the number above for information.

Days and Hours: Open daily.

Garden Type: Ornamental plantings along a flowing river within the city of San Antonio.

Garden Size: About two and a half miles of walkway, with many entrances and exits along the way.

The Gardens: Tropical and semitropical plantings reign here, with ferns, prostrate rosemaries, philodendrons, and such, providing the green backdrop for the gorgeous colors of hibiscus, crape myrtle, and lantana and the white highlights of caladium and camellia. Brugmansia, plumbago, redbud, variegated gingers, and wave after wave of brightly colored annuals bloom successively under tall cypress trees.

Don't-Miss Feature: Have lunch or dinner at one of the riverside cafes or enjoy a short riverboat cruise.

Tour Policy: Tours are self-guided. Just follow the river.

Driving Instructions: You can enter the Riverwalk anywhere along its 2½-mile stretch. Park downtown if you like; access at the Rivercenter Mall Lagoon is spectacular, or try Crockett, Alamo, Market, St. Mary's, or Commerce Street. You can also enter from the convention center and some hotels and restaurants. Alternatively, the King William Historic District offers access at Durango Boulevard.

San Antonio Botanical Garden

Lucille Halsell Conservatory
555 Funston Place at North New Braunfels
San Antonio, Texas 78209
210-207-3250
http://www.sabot.org

Fee: Adults $4; Seniors and Military $2; Children $1; Members free. Be sure to pick up a Visitor's Guide, which contains an invaluable map to the grounds.

Accessibility: Wide, smooth paths and a carefully planned layout make most of this garden highly accessible. Some of the outlying areas devoted to native gardens, replicating as they do the rocky or muddy environments from which the plants come, present more of a challenge. Wheelchairs are available at the front desk, and arrangements can be made to accommodate the needs of the hearing impaired by calling 210-207-3261 (TTY).

Days and Hours: Open every day except Christmas and New Year's Days. March-October from 9-6; November-February, doors close at 5. A restaurant in the visitor center is open Tuesday-Sunday from 11-2, and the gift shop keeps the same hours as the garden.

Garden Type: Botanical garden planted and maintained for the purposes of education and research, as well as the conservation and display of plants from around the world. Includes conservatory, display gardens, formal beds, and native plantings.

Garden Size: Thirty-three acres. Wear comfortable shoes; you're going to be here awhile.

Themes and Special Features: Butterfly Garden, Old-fashioned Cottage Garden, Rose Garden, Garden for the Blind, Wisteria Arbor, Sacred Garden, Japanese Garden, Herb Garden, daylily beds, spectacular conservatory, and displays of plants native to central, east, and southwest regions of Texas, along with three wooden buildings from the 19th century and two adobe structures.

The Gardens: If you're a real garden lover, plan to take some time to visit all the treasures here. This is an all-day excursion in almost any season except the dead of winter, and even then plant lovers will find beauty worth several hours' diversion.

Excellent signage throughout tempts you to pause and read not only each plant's identifying marker, but often whimsical or interesting (even educational) facts about different species. You'll learn, for instance, that the Japanese name for "crape myrtle" means "monkey slide down tree," a reference to the slick trunk of the mature tree. (Two wonderful examples stand beside the sign.) Signage extends to the daylily beds and rose plantings, a fact that gardeners appreciate when they fall in love with particular must-have specimens.

The water features and artwork that decorate the garden are chosen with restrained taste, enhancing the natural beauties without distracting attention from them. One particularly beautiful example is a bronze sculpture by Bob Guelich called "Fishing Lesson," depicting a mother heron feeding her two offspring. It stands in the Garden for the Blind, inviting exploration by touch.

The Garden for the Blind is an ambitious project designed to allow visitors to touch, rub, and smell a wide variety of fragrant or sensory plants within a small, easily accessible area. The waist-high beds contain such aromatic herbs as lemon verbena, scented geraniums, a variety of basils, lavender, and sweet bay. Rice paper plant and lamb's ear offer tactile treats, while camphor tree, vanilla shrub, star anise, and root beer plant perfume the air. Signs in both Braille and large block type identify many of the most popular plants.

The San Antonio Garden Center funds this garden and pays admission for visually handicapped visitors.

The Rose and Herb Gardens offer a special treat. Roses old and new erupt with color and perfume in spring and fall, and you will find many varieties in bloom most of the summer. The Herb Garden features a mint collection to delight young and old—pineapple, lime,

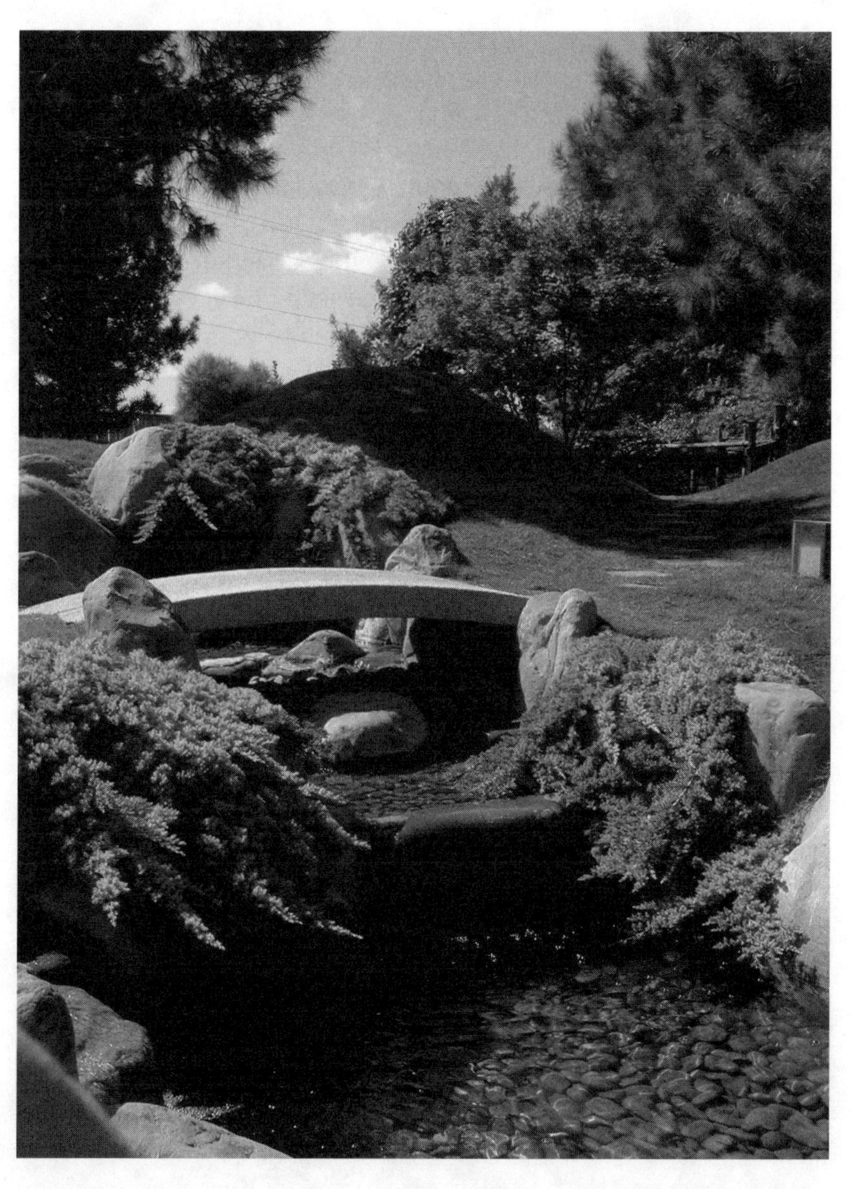

peppermint, and spearmint—and a thyme garden showing off the scents of grapefruit, lemon, coconut, caraway, and nutmeg thymes.

The Sacred Garden lets visitors wander among plants spoken of in the Bible or other sacred texts. Olive, oleander, pomegranate, and grape can all be found.

Lucile Halsell Conservatory: One of the most impressive garden structures you're ever likely to encounter, this 40,000-square-foot complex lies mostly underground, the ingenious architect's solution to the problem of insulating a greenhouse in such a hot, dry climate. The design allows seven different climate zones to be maintained independent of each other. Here, you will find plants indigenous to alpine regions, rain forests, deserts, and the tropics.

Five pyramid or cone-shaped glass structures catch your eye as you stroll toward the east side of the grounds. At the entry, the fragrance of rosemary envelopes the visitor, exuded by the five- to seven-foot-long draperies of prostrate rosemaries that cascade down the wall. On a hot day, the smell can be intoxicating. On a cold one, it will make you think of Christmas.

Inside, a wide, gentle tunnel leads the visitor to each of the protected environments, the Alpine Exhibit, featuring lewisia, sea pink, and edelweiss; the Epiphyte Display, full of orchids and bromeliads in the mist; an Aquatic Garden featuring lotus and other water-loving plants; the Desert Pavilion with its treasure house of cacti and succulents; the Hot Tropical Room displaying breadfruit, coffee, cacao, ginger, cardamom, and plumeria; the Palm House, 65 feet tall and full of palm trees of every variety imaginable (watch out for falling coconuts); to the Orangery in an uncovered courtyard, where, during summer months, orange trees vie for attention with macadamia trees, avocados, and allspice bushes. Here, you'll find the entrance to the Fern Room, a grotto sunken 28 feet into the ground to accommodate tall tree ferns, as well as cascades of climbing and flowering plants, including the vanilla orchid.

Kumamoto En: This garden within a garden re-creates the feeling of an authentic Japanese park, and well it might. It was designed and built by Japanese artists and craftsmen as a gift from San Antonio's sister city, Kumamoto, Japan. In fact, the designer, Mr. Kiyoshi Yasui, has been designated a national living treasure in his homeland for the creation of stunning works like this.

Beauty may indeed lie largely in the eye of the beholder, but some aesthetic values are surely universal, and they speak to all who enter here. Harmony of line, for instance, serenity that evokes a sense of timelessness. Nowhere, not even in the great gardens of Japan itself, have I seen the subtle grace of simplicity expressed more beautifully than in this gem of hidden complexities.

Authenticity is the key here, with styles of fencing and paving borrowed from several Japanese traditions, but it does not overshadow the symbolism always inherent in great works of art. You can stroll around the water features and back out the gate within a minute or two if you're so inclined, or you can study the stones and paths and bridges and islands, discovering the details that make the whole experience so much greater than the sum of the parts.

It helps to know that the garden's design represents a picture of the relationship between the two sister cities and their nations. The main body of water in the center symbolizes the great Pacific Ocean, and the bridge across it, friendship and cooperation. The large berm behind it, covered in emerald zoysia grass, represents the famous Mount Fujiyama itself.

Tea ceremonies are sometimes conducted in the azumaya or tea arbor, which in Japan is not a teahouse, but a place for people to sit in reflection or meditation before partaking in a tea ceremony. Four benches inside are placed so that waiting people do not face each other and thus risk distraction from their spiritual preparations.

Bird Alert: In the summer, look for black-bellied whistling ducks and wood ducks on the lake at the north end of the park. Other ducks will show up during the winter. Black-chinned hummingbirds may be busy among the flowers from very early spring until late October.

Sponsored Activities: People like to have fun here. Families are always welcome, especially during the annual two-day Viva Botanica celebration in the spring and the Gardens by Moonlight event in the fall. Music, games, ethnic foods, horticultural presentations, and special exhibits turn the garden into a fiesta twice a year, inviting all to share the wonders of this special garden. Plant sales held throughout the year offer a chance to pick up the newest introductions or the best-adapted plants for the xeric landscape.

Classes, seminars, workshops, and other events go on throughout the year. Call the Special Events line at 210-207-3255 for information about what will be happening while you're here.

Tours and Rentals: Tours for 20 or more can be arranged, with a fee of $3 for adults and fifty cents per child. You can make arrangements for special tours or find out about educational programs by calling 210-207-3255. For information about renting sites for meetings or weddings, call 210-829-0804.

Volunteer and Support Opportunities: The San Antonio Botanical Society is the nonprofit support organization for the Botanical Garden, and they welcome new members and volunteers. Membership brings involvement in the many society projects, including members-only events. It provides free admission to the garden, a 10 percent discount at the gift shop, and four yearly issues of the society's newsletter. members also get a fee reduction to some seminars and classes offered by the gardens.

Gift Shop: The Garden Gate Gift Shop is open daily and offers a sophisticated selection of gifts and books related to gardening and native wildlife (210-829-1227). All sales revenue goes to support the San Antonio Botanical Society projects.

The Carriage House Kitchen presents an array of freshly prepared luncheon choices every day except Monday (210-821-6447).

Driving Instructions: From IH-35 north of downtown, take the North New Braunfels exit and go north to Parland and turn right (east).

If you're coming from San Antonio International Airport, take Highway 281 south and exit at Hildebrand. Go east (left) on

Hildebrand to North New Braunfels and turn south (right). At Parland, turn east (left).

Schultze House Cottage Garden

514 Hemisfair Park
San Antonio, Texas 78205
210-229-9161

Fee: Free.

Accessibility: Good.

Days and Hours: Open daily during daylight hours.

Garden Type: Cottage garden.

Garden Size: Less than an acre.

Themes and Special Features: Plantings featuring historical periods, xeriscape conditions, shade tropicals, herbs, and bulbs.

The Gardens: Bexar County Master Gardeners designed and planted this garden to show homeowners and visitors how to maintain a colorful landscape in a thirsty environment without wasted effort or water. They maintain it still and run the gift shop. The base of the garden is heirloom, pass along plants that have proven their survival value—old roses, bulbs, lilies, and reseeding annuals like moss rose and zinnia. It heartens even the most faint-hearted of gardeners to see what can be done with these old fail-safe beauties.

Gift Shop: Quartered in the 1893 house, which was restored for Hemisfair in 1967, the well-stocked shop is open from 10 until 4 Tuesday through Saturday.

Sponsored Activities: Monthly brown-bag lunch seminars; call for a current schedule.

Tour and Rental Policies: Tours are self-guided. Plants are well labeled. Weddings, receptions, reunions, and other special events can be accommodated here with enough advance planning. Call San Antonio Parks and Recreation Reservations Service at 210-207-7275.

Volunteer and Support Opportunities: Call 210-467-6575 for information about the Bexar County Master Gardeners.

Driving Instructions: From IH-37, follow the signs to Hemisfair Park. The house and garden are between the Federal Courthouse and the Tower of the Americas.

Finding More Flowers in Central Texas

Austin

October is herb time in Austin, as the Austin Herb Society and Area Garden Council hold their annual Austin HerbFest at Zilker Botanical Gardens, 2220 Barton Springs Road. There is a small admission fee, but the festival is well worth the price. Call 512-477-8672 for this year's dates.

The Austin Pond Society hosts a spectacular tour of water gardens on private property, usually in June. To find out this year's dates, call 512-896-6377.

Display gardens for the Daylily Society (American Hemerocallis Society) will be open to the public in two cities in late spring. In Austin, call Richard and Anna Marie Rosen, 512-331-0243, to ascertain the dates and other details. In San Antonio, call Colonel and Mrs. Michael M. Conrad, 210-492-1114.

Barton Springs Nursery in Austin maintains display gardens showing the use of Hill Country native plants in the landscape. You will find it at 3601 Bees Cave Road, open seven days a week. The phone number is 512-328-6655.

Kerrville

Riverside Nature Center sponsors a spring tour of private gardens. Get the details for this year at 830-257-4837.

San Antonio

The Antique Rose Emporium has opened a store at 7561 East Evans Road. The display gardens are worth seeing. Call 210-651-4565 for information.

Part Five

The Gardens of South Texas

Alamo, Aransas Pass, Brookshire, Corpus Christi, Galveston, Hempstead, Houston, McAllen-Lower Rio Grande Valley, Rockport-Fulton, Victoria, Weslaco

"No one dreams the gardens to be found in Texas without seeing them firsthand."

Julie Ryan, *Perennial Gardens for Texas*

It's when you drive through the area south of San Antonio that you finally begin to understand just how big Texas really is. Mile after mile of dry-looking brush country, some 21 million acres of it, is not hospitable to what we think of as garden plants. Once you get used to the absence of green and become attuned to the nuances of the landscapes, though, you will begin to see the beauty in native grasses, especially in fall and winter, and appreciate the occasional live oak or mesquite when you encounter it.

To the east, coastal prairie grass supports an enormous cattle industry, and far to the south, heavy or sandy soils give way to the deep delta soil of the Rio Grande. Here, the finger of frost is rarely felt, and industry thrives on citrus and vegetable crops. Hidalgo County leads the state in the cash value of its farm crops, which also include sugar cane, grain, and cotton. On the coast, the petrochemical industry flourishes.

In the Lower Rio Grande valley, palms, citrus, poinsettias, and bougainvillea lend an exotic air year round, and you'll enjoy driving the long, straight highways through fields of melons, tomatoes, corn, or oranges. The small city of Mission is home to the American Poinsettia Society's headquarters and celebrates that fact every December with a Poinsettia Show. In January the town celebrates being the home of Texas ruby red grapefruit, too, with a week-long Texas Citrus Festival.

A serious freeze is a rare event in the southernmost reaches of this area, allowing householders to landscape with what the rest of the state considers "house plants," like pothos, or devil's ivy, tropical hibiscus, asparagus fern, and citrus trees. Brilliant bougainvillea reaches astounding heights, and flowering shrubs grow into trees.

The coastal cities offer a spectacular rose garden in Victoria, the most beautiful formal estate garden in Texas in Houston, hummingbird gardens in Rockport, rain forests in Galveston, and orchids in

Corpus Christi. Check out the cactus garden in Alamo, the water lilies in Brookshire, and the Butterfly Festival in Mission.

And everywhere you travel, keep your eye peeled for birds. At least three-fourths of the 600 birds Texas is known to harbor can be spotted here at one time or another. Naturally, people come from all over the world to bird this area, particularly in sites along the coastline and in the Lower Rio Grande Valley.

The Great Texas Coastal Birding Trail, a series of looping trails leading into productive birding sites along the coast, is mapped out and maintained by Texas Parks and Wildlife and Texas Department of Transportation for your convenience. You will need copies of the maps the state provides if you are to make the most of the birding opportunities along the trail. Some locations are on privately held land. The maps tell you when each site is open to the public, how accessible it is, what birds to look for, and how to get from one part of the loop to the next. Pick up maps at the Chamber of Commerce of any city along the coast from Beaumont to the Rio Grande River. Call 1-888-TXBIRDS, or request maps by email at birdingtrails@tpwd.state.tx.us.

Alamo

Sunderland's Cactus Garden

Route 1, Box 40
Alamo, Texas 78516 (see Driving Instructions below)
956-787-2040

Fee: Free.

Accessibility: Good.

Days and Hours: 9-5 Monday-Friday. Tours can be arranged for Sunday mornings.

Garden Type: Wholesale and retail nursery.

Garden Size: Five acres, including retail and display areas.

Themes and Special Features: The beauty of cacti, both native and exotic, and petrified wood.

The Gardens: Thousands upon thousands of desert plants live and thrive in this natural rock garden setting, representing about 2,000 different kinds of cacti. The gardeners propagate them on site, thus preserving rare and endangered species. Stroll among them and pick out the ones you like. They have enough to sell you some.

Don't-Miss Feature: The 25-foot tall *Packycereus pringlii* is supposed to be the largest nursery-grown cactus in the whole state. Ironically, this mighty specimen is not a native Texan, but an import from Baja, California.

Bird Alert: You are standing in the midst of what veteran birders have proclaimed one of the twelve best birding spots in the country. Some 460 species are regularly sighted in this region, including 34 that are not seen anywhere else in the U.S.A. The Rio Grande Valley Audubon Society maintains a hotline for reporting or learning about sightings: 956-969-2731. You can also get information about birds from the Santa Ana Wildlife Refuge. Their number is 956-787-3079.

Tour Policy: Tours are generally self-guided. But you can make an appointment for a lecture tour for your group (held on Sunday mornings only) by calling ahead.

Driving Instructions: Sunderland's lies less than a mile north of the town of Alamo where Farm Road 907 intersects with Farm Road 495.

Aransas Pass

Newbury Park Hummingbird Garden

Aransas Pass Chamber of Commerce
130 W. Goodnight
Aransas Pass, Texas 78336
361-758-2750; 800-633-3028
email: info@aransaspass.org
http://www.aransaspass.org

Fee: Free.

Accessibility: Excellent.

Days and Hours: Open daily.

Garden Type: Small community park developed by the city, in cooperation with Texas Parks and Wildlife and Texas Department of Transportation, as a hummingbird garden.

The Garden: Mature specimens of sure-fire hummingbird favorites lure the little guys in reliably, especially during September migration. This garden offers the chance to get up close and personal with everyone's favorite bird. Most will be ruby-throated, though buff-bellied, black-chinned, and rufous are also possible.

Bird Alert: You are in the heart of a birder's paradise here. There's almost no telling what you might spot. Both spring and fall migrations present opportunities to add to your life list. If you plan to spend much time in this area, be sure to bring a good bird identification guide.

Driving Instructions: The park is located on Lamont Street, just off Business 35, near that highway's intersection with Loop 90. Watch for signs.

The Hummingbird as Predator

One of the most common denizens of the public garden and everyone's favorite wild bird, the hummingbird, amuses and delights young and old. It can fly upside down and backwards or hover in midair like a helicopter. Its iridescent plumage catches the light and reflects it back to the eye of the beholder in a flash of brilliant color, and its tiny wings beat through the air with a thrum that turns heads. It has often been called a flying jewel, a symbol of energy as beauty.

But let spiders, caterpillars, aphids, and ants beware. If a creature is small enough to swallow, hummingbirds will eat it.

Once thought to feed strictly on nectar from flowers, hummers are now known to indulge in much broader appetites. In fact, they will dive into a hovering swarm of insects and snatch up prey or use their wings to blow dry leaves into the air and then glean insect or spider eggs off the undersides. They have even been known to steal a meal right out of a spider's web.

Despite their newfound reputation as meat eaters, hummingbirds still depend on flowers for much of their food, so they delight in public gardens and other plantings. The flowers they prefer tend to be vibrant colored, often tubular shaped, and usually without much scent. Fragrance would encourage competition from other nectar feeders, so most plants that have specialized in using hummingbirds as pollinators don't have it. Salvias of all colors, trumpet vine, coral vine, lantana, honeysuckle, and other native plants lure hummingbirds into yards and gardens all over the state.

The species of hummingbirds you're most likely to encounter in Texas gardens include ruby-throated, black-chinned, buff-bellied, broad-tailed, blue-throated, rufous, Anna's, calliope, magnificent, and Lucifer. Other species that have been sighted in the state at one time or another include Costa's, green violet-ear,

Allen's, violet-crowned, white-eared, green-breasted mango, broad-billed, and Berylline.

Hummers will come into yards and gardens, attracted by artificial feeders. But don't let anyone sell you a hummingbird house. They don't use them.

Join the Texas Parks and Wildlife Hummingbird Roundup

Are you fascinated by the behavior of hummingbirds in your own Texas yard and garden? Why not be an official hummingbird observer and help the state wildlife department gather more facts about the range and habits of these little birds? You can do so by participating in an ongoing survey that asks you to record what you see in your own area. You can download the survey form from the Internet, or you can order it as part of a Roundup Kit from Texas Parks and Wildlife. With the kit, for $6, you get not only the survey form, but several other goodies: some scarlet sage seeds for attracting hummers; a calendar for recording sightings; information about identifying species, cleaning feeders, and planting nectar plants; news about hummingbird-related events; and an annual newsletter.

Learn all about it at www.tpwd.state.tx.us/nature/birding/humrunup.htm, or contact the department directly:

Texas Backyard Hummingbird Survey
Wildlife Diversity Program
Texas Parks and Wildlife
4200 Smith School Road
Austin, Texas 78744
512-389-4800

Brookshire

Lilypons Water Gardens

839 FM 1489
Brookshire, TX 77423-0188
800-999-5459
email: info@lilypons.com
http://www.lilypons.com

Lilypons Water Gardens

 **Fee:** Free.

Accessibility: Very good.

Days and Hours: March-September: 9:30-5:30 Monday-Saturday; 11-5:30 Sunday. Closed Easter Sunday and July 4. October-February: 9:30-4:30 Monday-Saturday; closed Sundays, Thanksgiving Day, and December 24-January 1.

Garden Type: Retail and production nursery for water gardens, selling plants, ponds, fish, and supplies.

Garden Size: Twenty acres, including production and retail; the display area you will tour is probably about half an acre.

Themes and Special Features: It's all about water here, what grows in it or near it. If water features beguile you, or if you want to see the range of products possible for the water-loving homeowner, this place is a real education.

The Gardens: It's a delight to wander about the retail grounds and take in the displays this company uses to merchandise its water-related products. Literally dozens of working fountains, springs, and burblers enliven the atmosphere, from minuscule to huge, all hosting different plants, some in bloom, many showing off ornamental foliage.

Don't-Miss Feature: Around back, you'll glimpse greenhouses and ponds, where workers produce enormous numbers of water lilies to be shipped all over the nation.

Bird Alert: All kinds of shorebirds can be expected here. You may catch a little blue heron or a snowy egret foraging among the ponds. Overhead, look for white-tailed hawk, crested caracara or, in winter, peregrine falcon.

Sponsored Activities: Renaissance Festival on weekends in October. Lilypons Days the third weekend in June. Koi and Wine Festival on Labor Day weekend.

Tour Policy: Tours are self-guided, or a sales person will be glad to show you around. Group tours can be arranged by calling 281-391-0076. Remember, though, that this is a working retail establishment, and personnel may be quite busy during spring and early summer.

Driving Instructions: The hamlet of Brookshire is located west of Houston on IH-10. Take exit 731 and turn south on Farm Road 1489. Slow down, because the place you're looking for is less than two blocks away, on your left.

Corpus Christi

Corpus Christi Botanical Gardens

8545 South Staples
Corpus Christi, Texas 78413
361-852-2100
http://www.ccbotanicalgardens.org

Fee: Ages 12-65 $3; ages 5-11 $2.50; over 65 or under 5 $1.50; Members free.

Accessibility: Good.

Days and Hours: 9-5 Tuesday-Sunday.

Garden Type: Combination botanical garden, with both highly cultivated exhibits and nature trail featuring native plants and wildlife.

Garden Size: One hundred eighty acres, including extensive natural areas.

Themes and Special Features: Collections include orchids, plumerias, roses, hibiscus, tropicals, and water plants, as well as a bird and butterfly trail and a cottage garden. A sensory garden stimulates all the senses.

The Gardens: The folks here intend to make this a garden to take seriously, and they are off to a good start. Still young and growing, the gardens are taking shape with an impressive mix of exotic, imported plants with lots of beautiful natives and old-fashioned adapted perennials, like roses.

Don't-Miss Feature: Here they hold what may be the largest orchid collection in Texas that's open to the public. About 2,500 plants bloom in memoriam of their benefactor Don Larkin, who left some 2,000 of the plants to the Gardens in his will.

Bird Alert: Shorebirds, waders, and waterfowl will dominate here, but watch for groove-billed ani and pyrrhuloxia, too, as well as Bewick's wren and white-eyed vireo. Roseate spoonbill is always fun. And I'll bet you didn't know that white pelicans are really that BIG!

Sponsored Activities: A Children's Garden in spring and fall is a hands-on project to teach kids to grow vegetables. A Wilderness Camp entertains them in the summer while you wait for the big October plant sale. There will be an even bigger sale, and a festival too, in April.

Gift Shop: A well-designed and stocked little store offers books, stationery, ceramics, and other arts and crafts, many of them handmade by the garden's Craft Guild.

Tour Policy: Tours are self-guided. Pick up a map in the Visitor Center.

Volunteer and Support Opportunities: The money you pay for admission or membership plus grants and donations funds this garden, not tax money. Memberships start at $50. Volunteer opportunities abound here. If you like to be outdoors, work with children, get involved in construction, tell people about plants, or help host special events, they will find a job for you.

Driving Instructions: From South Padre Island Drive (State Highway 358), exit at Staples and head south for about 4½ miles. Watch for the green signs.

Galveston

Moody Gardens Rain Forest Pyramid

One Hope Boulevard
(see Driving Instructions below)
Galveston, Texas 77554
800-582-4673
http://www.moodygardens.com

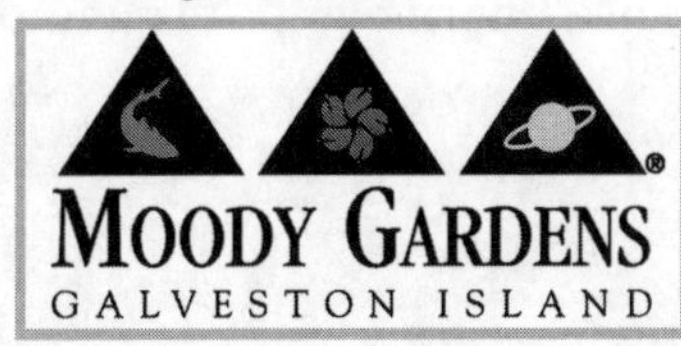

$ **Fee:** Adult $8.95; Children 4-12 $5.95; Seniors 65 and over $6.95. Fees do not include admission to attractions other than the Rain Forest.

Accessibility: Excellent. Watch for a sign for the handicap drop-off ramp near the Visitor Center.

Days and Hours: Open 10-6 Sunday-Thursday, 10-8 Friday-Saturday.

Garden Type: Glass conservatory, re-creating conditions in the world's rain forests. Includes plants, fish, butterflies, birds, bats, and insects from American, Asian, and African rain forests. A 250-square-foot bat cave houses some 60 bats. A thick glass window into their hanging boudoir lets you observe a wide range of activities.

Garden Size: Ten-stories, home to thousands of flora and fauna.

Themes and Special Features: Birds live loose here. Newly metamorphosed butterflies are released into the air from the Hatching Hut twice a day, at 11 and 2. You may see an African violet growing out of a crack in a rock that looks just like one your grandmother has in a pot in her living room. Piranha and other fish indigenous to rain forest habitats swim in the streams.

The Gardens: Moody Gardens is a colossal entertainment complex, encompassing three IMAX Theaters, including the kind with moving seats, a huge aquarium, beaches, restaurants, a 300-room hotel, boat rides, and three brightly colored, pyramid-shaped buildings that dominate the flat coastal plain for miles around.

It also has the most drop-dead gorgeous parking lot you will ever lay eyes on. And they don't even seem to know it. They must take all those enormous palms and oleanders and hibiscus and other exotic

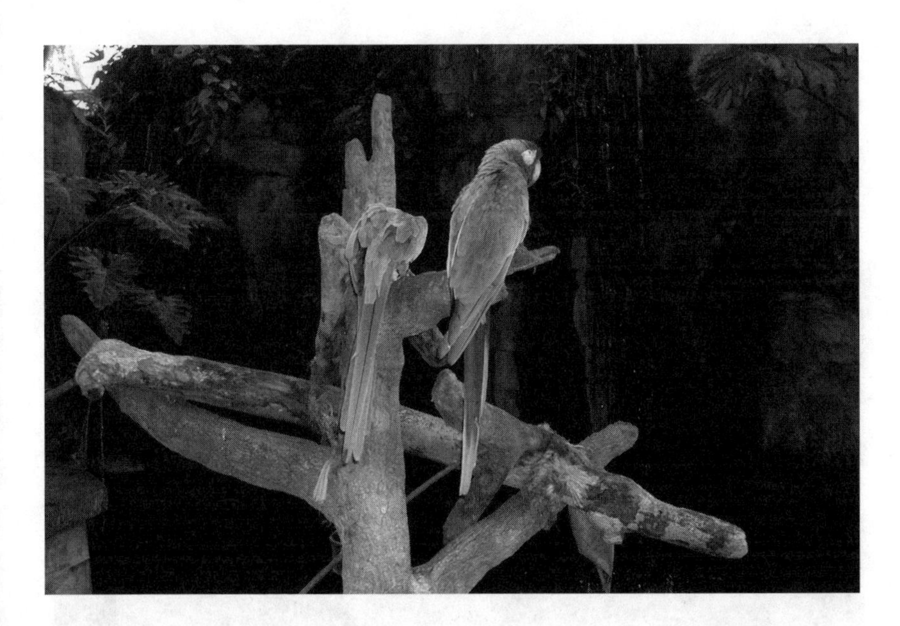

bloomery and shrubbery entirely for granted, I suppose. The exotic beauty of this place knocked me off my feet. These outdoor plantings and the Rain Forest Pyramid are what we will concern ourselves with here. But if you bring kids onto this property, don't expect to get away without exploring some of the other wonders, too.

After you've gawked around the parking lot for a while, leave the car in one of the many spots available and stroll through the grounds. Pass the ten-foot-tall turk's cap. Take a photo of a Medjool date palm. Meander down smooth concrete paths on the south and east sides of the Visitor Center. Enjoy the spectacular water features on the bay side. Sit on the terrace and catch your breath before you venture inside.

If you've followed me here, you're now at the rear entrance to the Visitor Center. As you enter, look ahead and to your right for the first of many treats—pink flamingoes viewed through a window into their rain forest habitat. That's a taste of the good things to come, but you must buy your tickets first, so head to your left and toward the front of the building to the ticket stand before returning to enter the Rain Forest Pyramid.

Don't-Miss Feature: The bat cave has to be the most exotic attraction here, but the biological diversity is mind-boggling. A multitude of orchid species decorates the stone walls in the American Forest, joined by bromeliads, gingers, and ferns in the Asian Forest and ficus, ebony, and mahogany trees in the African Forest.

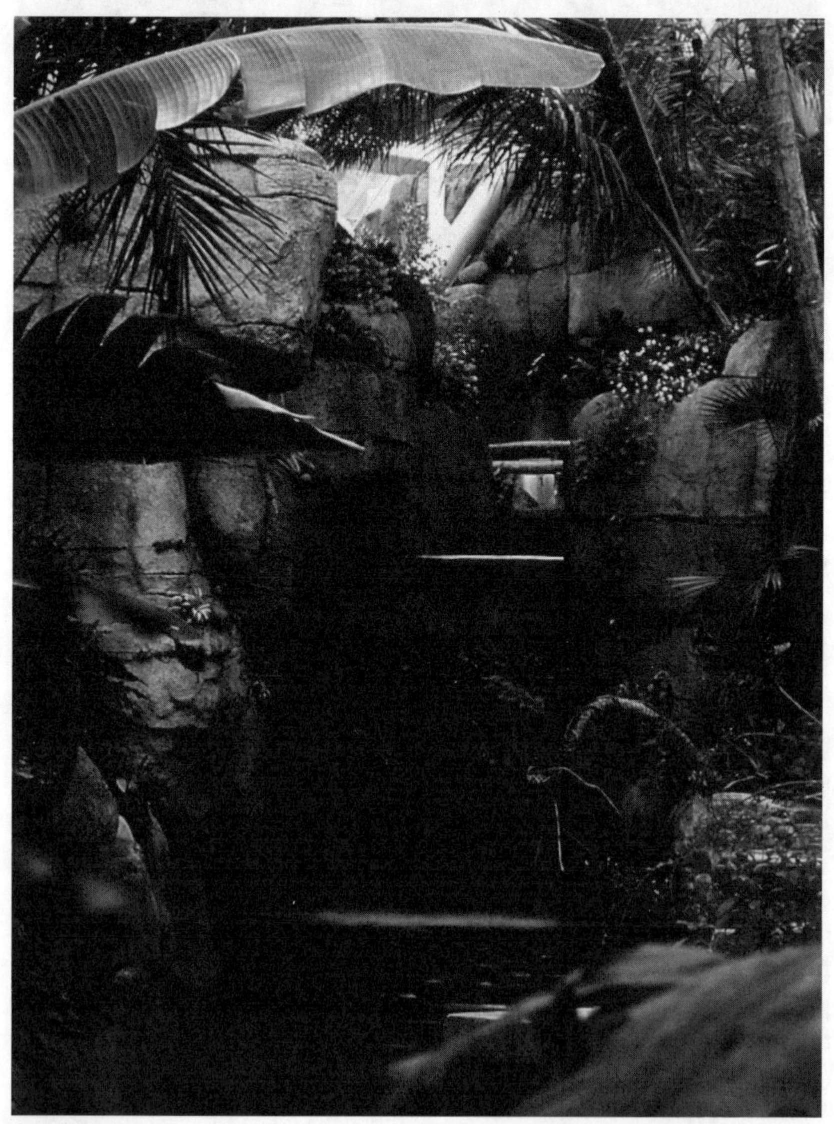

Bird Alert: Yes, be alert. The birds are very tame and you don't want to stumble over one in your path. Also, as dusk comes on, both birds and butterflies start settling into roosts for the night, so try to respect their privacy and not startle them as they doze.

Sponsored Activities: The range of children's activities here is both original and challenging and includes day camps and sleepovers that allow children to explore the pyramids more fully. Reservations and prepayment are necessary. Call 409-744-4673, extension 4325. Scouting activities and birthday parties can also be hosted here.

Gift Shop/Restaurant: Nature's Wonders is the store in the Visitor Center, and it is all that it should be for such a first-class operation as Moody Gardens. You'll find a prodigious selection of gifts, apparel, and toys, though not many books, featuring the kinds of natural attractions you've come here to see. As for refreshments, the Garden Restaurant offers an elegant eating opportunity at reasonable prices, and a snack bar in the lobby stocks regulation fast fare.

Tour Policy: Tours are self-guided. Special rates for groups of more than 20 can be arranged with two weeks notice.

Volunteer and Support Opportunities: A Moody Gardens membership gives you a full year's admission to all attractions, as well as substantial discounts in the gift shops, restaurant, and hotel. Individual membership is $85; family membership for up to five is $260.

Driving Instructions: You will cross over onto Galveston Island on IH-45 South. Take Exit 1A at 61st Street. At the light, turn right onto 61st, then right onto Stewart Road. When that road splits, continue straight ahead on Jones Drive. Turn right into the gardens at the sign.

When you get ready to leave this place, make a point to drive over to the Moody Gardens Hotel on the southeast side of the grounds first, and from the parking lot, get a look at the "hanging gardens" planted on top of the hotel.

Hempstead

Peckerwood Garden

Route 3, Box 103
Hempstead, Texas 77445
979-826-3232
email: info@peckerwoodgarden.com
http://www.peckerwoodgarden.com

Fee: Yes. See Days and Hours below.

Accessibility: Limited. Call ahead.

Days and Hours: Peckerwood Garden is open to the general public only during specific days each year, usually the third weekend of the month from March through November. Contact them for specific dates and times. The fee is $5 and no reservations are required. Children under 12 are not allowed in the garden. For a fee, private tours for groups and individuals can be arranged throughout the year to provide substantial information about the history of the garden and the botanical significance of its contents.

Garden Type: Private research garden now operating as an independent nonprofit foundation.

Garden Size: Twelve acres.

Themes and Special Features: Rare plants, some of them no longer growing in the wild; plants collected from mountain ranges of Mexico; flora being tested for use in the horticulture industry.

The Gardens: Designed by artist John Fairey, the gardens are laid out as wandering woodland trails along the banks of a spring-fed stream, with dedicated beds for dryland plants and unique ornamentals. Magnolia, gum, oak, holly, and other trees provide a canopy. Outdoor sculpture and collections of folk art from the U.S. and Mexico lend added color and charm. The effect is one of astonishing beauty.

Don't-Miss Feature: Visit Yucca Do, the affiliated nursery next door, to purchase many of the plants you see here.

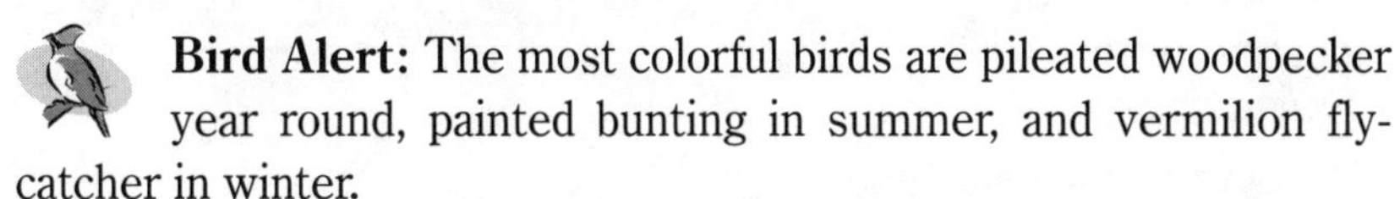

Bird Alert: The most colorful birds are pileated woodpecker year round, painted bunting in summer, and vermilion flycatcher in winter.

Sponsored Activities: Forums and symposia of interest to artistic and horticultural communities are held yearly. Most are pretty esoteric, but if serious discussions of art and culture are your cup of tea, call for a current schedule.

Tour Policy: See Days and Hours above.

Volunteer and Support Opportunities: The Garden Foundation depends on the direct support of interested citizens. All proceeds from seed sales, garden tours, workshops, and memberships go directly to the nonprofit organization. Memberships are available in a range from $25 to $2,000, with appropriate benefits for each level. Gift memberships are also available.

Driving Instructions: From U.S. Business Highway 290 in Hempstead, take Farm Road 359 south about a mile and a half to its intersection with Farm Road 3346. Watch for Yucca Do Nursery on the west side of the road and park there.

Houston

Bayou Bend

1 Westcott Street
Houston, Texas 77007-7009
713-639-7750
http://www.bayoubend.uh.edu

MFA **H** *Bayou Bend Collection and Gardens*

Fee: Adult $3, Children under 11 free, Garden only. House tours are extra.

Accessibility: Variable, but mostly quite good. For wheelchair access, approach the house from Lazy Lane, off Kirby Drive. If you will need help, call ahead.

Days and Hours: 10-5 Tuesday-Saturday; 1-5 Sunday, garden only. House hours differ.

Garden Type: Estate garden surrounding a 28-room mansion.

Garden Size: Fourteen acres.

Themes and Special Features: Eight graceful formal gardens introduce you to the site. Explore them and then follow acres of winding paths through beautiful natural settings full of unexpected delights. Children will love the topiary garden featuring small green shrubs clipped into the shapes of native animals, including a turkey. Any homeowner in search of design ideas or plant material for a heavily shaded landscape will find infinite inspiration along the woodland paths here.

The Gardens: This estate was the home of Ima Hogg, daughter of Texas governor Jim Hogg; she lived here from 1929 until 1965. In 1957 she donated the house and grounds to the Houston Museum of Fine Arts. The house holds one of the nation's premier collections of American art and antiques and as such, is a museum well worth visiting. But the gardens easily hold their own in such a rarified atmosphere.

Bayou Bend is a creek with ravines draining into it, which work together to create a dramatic backdrop for one of the most beautiful

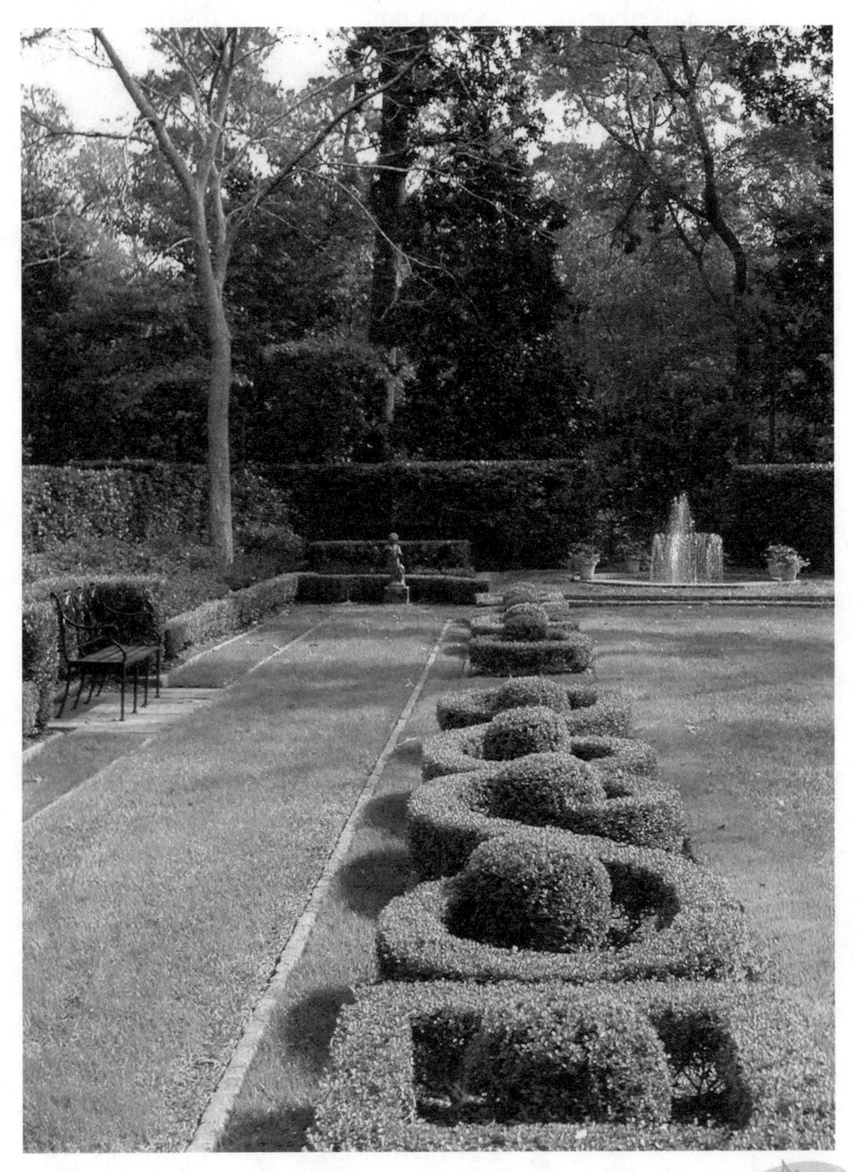

shade gardens you will ever see. Ferns, liriope, and ophiopogon anchor the understory for slopes full of dogwood, redbud, and magnolia, while pines, oaks, and elms arch over all. The paths here just seem to go on and on, with each corner you turn revealing new vistas of loveliness and enough nooks and crannies to please the most intrepid explorer. Go far enough and you will discover the White Garden, where something white is almost always in bloom.

The formal gardens feature Carrara marble statues of Roman goddesses, imported from Italy, which set the tone for the setting dedicated to them. Clio, Muse of History, and Euterpe, Muse of Music, oversee geometrical beds edged in severely clipped boxwood and the tiny ophiopogon the Japanese call "Dragon's Mustache," where fig ivy clings like skin to walls and wisteria is trained in tree form and kept strictly in bounds.

Diana the Huntress dominates a garden of her own. Japanese yews form a magnificent backdrop for the statue and set off the trees and shrubs that bloom in pink throughout the seasons—magnolias, azaleas, and crape myrtles. And in Euterpe's Garden, the Japanese yews are hewed into giant cylinders and pink blooms predominate again.

Throughout the formal gardens, azaleas, magnolias, and camellias range in color from pale to deep pink and red, their effect finding its most whimsical expression in the Butterfly Garden, where evergreen azaleas clipped in the shape of butterfly wings blaze with four shades of color in early spring.

Don't-Miss Feature: If you look closely, you will find tree stumps along the woodland path, petrified into a tranquil, jewel-like beauty.

Bird Alert: The woods are thick here, and even though you are in the middle of a great city, there will be bird life. Stay alert for pileated and red-bellied woodpeckers anytime of the year, joined in winter by yellow-bellied sapsucker, ruby-crowned kinglet, and yellow-rumped warbler and in summer by white-eyed vireo and ruby-throated hummingbird.

Sponsored Activities: Bayou Bend is always featured on the Azalea Trail held in March by the River Oaks Garden Club.

Tour Policy: Tours of the garden can be self-guided with the help of a map you pick up at the Visitor Center. If you want more in-depth information about the garden, in particular about the history of its development, look into one of the regular tours given by the River Oaks Garden Club. Cost is reasonable and may include the estate house if you wish. Group and school tours can also be arranged. Call 713-639-7750.

Volunteer and Support Opportunities: Contact the River Oaks Garden Club at 713-523-2483.

Driving Instructions: You may want to study the area on a city map before you start out, or call the Gardens for detailed instructions. The grounds lie south of Memorial Drive on Westcott Street, west of downtown. You can take Memorial west from downtown or Westcott south from IH-10. Park in the lot and take the footbridge across the bayou to the house.

Ima Hogg Yes, Ura Hogg No

As a child, I was told in all earnestness by people who should have known better that Governor Hogg had two daughters and named them Ima and Ura in a kind of creative defiance of all who found his family name amusing. That this story was apocryphal I did not discover until some forty years after first hearing it.

Apparently, the truth is that he had only one daughter and that he either couldn't hear the pun in the name he gave her or didn't think it was important. He took the name Ima from a poem his brother had written about the Civil War. It must have sounded poetic and heroic to him, a respectable name for a strong woman.

And she was that, though not without trial, spending her childhood as a musical prodigy, never marrying, and for a period needing the care of mental health professionals. I've sometimes wondered how much the name helped shape the person she became.

Born into a wealthy family noted for its public service, she was already a grown woman when oil was found on her family property, allowing her to develop her true philanthropic muscle. Music and other fine arts became her beneficiaries. Honors for her contributions to America's cultural heritage became the hallmarks of her long and productive life. But her gifts also reflected a continuing concern for people suffering "nervous disorders." Brilliantly educated and artistically gifted, she helped define America's perceptions of art and beauty from the home she built in Houston, surrounded with a formal garden, and bequeathed to the people as a museum.

In 1927 Ima Hogg must have looked around the wilderness woods growing on a bend in a Houston bayou and envisioned a world-class formal garden of exquisite design, clothed in shades of pink, lilac, and blue. It took her until 1942 to bring that vision to completion. Today the gardens at Bayou Bend remain one of this great lady's most beloved legacies.

Another family property donated to the state by Miss Ima is now the **Varner-Starr Plantation State Historical Park** in West Columbia. The house is situated on 65 acres along Varner Creek, about 50 miles south of Houston. Built on an 1824 Mexican land grant, this estate has seen much of what we call the history of Texas, having once briefly been the site for a holding cell for Santa Anna and having seen the first capital of Texas established nearby. The focus of this very popular tourist site is history, as you might guess, but you will see some attempt here to re-create and maintain flora that has been historically meaningful through the 150 years that people have gardened here.

To reach the park from West Columbia, drive north on Farm Road 2853. More information is available by calling 979-345-4656.

"What greater praise can be given than to say that one has been a good steward, transmitting the beauty of the past to a future which will perhaps sorely need such qualities?"

William C. Welch, *Antique Roses for the South*

Cockrell Butterfly Center at the Houston Museum of Natural Science

One Hermann Circle Drive
Houston, Texas 77030
713-639-4629
http://www.hmns.org

Fee: Prices for the Cockrell Center range from $3 for members to $5 for a regular adult. Admission to other exhibits and the IMAX Theater is not included.

Accessibility: The building is fully accessible throughout. Wheelchairs available. TTY pay phone in the Grand Hall. Handicap parking on the street and on every level of the parking garage.

Days and Hours: 9-6 Monday-Saturday; 11-6 Sunday. Closed Thanksgiving Day, Christmas Day, and the first Saturday in March.

Garden Type: Conservatory built and maintained especially as a living exhibit of butterflies. This is only one of many exhibits and educational entertainments available in this large museum. You will need at least an hour in the butterfly center.

Garden Size: Three-story, cone-shaped glass conservatory.

Themes and Special Features: Here, butterflies are king. Watch your step. They like to sun themselves wherever the urge strikes. If you want some of these flying jewels to check you out up close and personal, wear your brightest colors.

The Gardens: Featuring mostly plants of Central American provenance, this garden exists solely to create a beautiful natural setting for live butterflies to show off their charms. Strikes you as the perfect child amuser, doesn't it? Well it is, but you will be hooked, too, as, what seem to be, thousands of winged beauties flitter and flutter about, feeding on nectar from blooming plants or special feeders. Some of the flora here include mahogany, ironwood, palms, gingers, orchids, bromeliads, guava, coffee tree, and many others. Although they all sound exotic to me, quite a few of the flowering plants are feasible for growing in Houston-area landscapes, so take notes if you want to attract butterflies to your local garden.

Don't-Miss Feature: You may catch a glimpse of an iguana resting in a sunny spot. And make a special point to check out the exhibit of larvae and pupae. You only thought you knew all about metamorphosis.

Tour Policy: Self-guided tours start every quarter hour. All school groups must make advance reservations by calling 713-639-4629. Other groups of 20 or more may receive discounts by making reservations at the same number. The TTY number is 713-639-4687.

Gift Shop: Right next door to the conservatory, you will find a treasure house of butterfly-themed gifts, apparel, books, and study projects, along with lots of other great nature-related stuff. They're open the same hours as the butterfly center. The number is 713-639-4783.

Volunteer and Support Opportunities: This whole museum exists without either state or federal funding. Contributions from private and corporate citizens have built it and are even now steering it toward preeminence in the field of popular natural science. Since they depend on people like you to keep their doors open, they've made it easy for you to support their efforts. Memberships start at $45 for an individual, which brings unlimited admission to the museum exhibit hall for one or two people and a discount on IMAX, butterfly center, and planetarium tickets, and classes and VIP events. You get a newsletter, of course, plus all kinds of members-only special treatment. There are five more levels of support, all the way up to the President's Circle, which is pretty rarified territory, indeed, but only calls for a $1,000 contribution. For information about how you can support the museum, call 713-639-4617.

Driving Instructions: The museum is located in Hermann Park in the southwest region of the city off Main Street, near Rice University, Texas Medical Center, and the Museum District. If you are coming from the north on U.S. Highway 59, take Fannin Street south. Find the second lane from the left and stay in it until you reach the park. If you're coming from the west on U.S. 59, exit at Richmond and follow it east to Fannin and turn right (south). Stay in the second lane from the left until you reach the park. The museum building will be on your left. There is parking on the street. In the museum's large parking garage, the fee is $3.

River Oaks Garden Club Garden and Azalea Trail

2503 Westheimer
Houston, Texas 77098
713-523-2483
http://www.riveroaksgardenclub.org

Fee: Free.

Accessibility: Excellent.

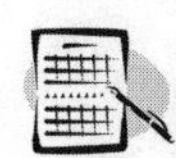

Days and Hours: Open to the public during regular business hours.

Garden Type: Classic old world formal garden.

Garden Size: About an acre.

Themes and Special Features: The River Oaks Garden Club acquired this 1880s building and its grounds in 1942. It's called the

Forum of Civics Building and now serves as headquarters for the Garden Society, itself a member of the Garden Club of America. The theme here is the configuration of plants and structures appropriate to a formal and historic landscape.

The Gardens: Small, very formal, with ivy arches, clipped hedges, huge crape myrtles, colorful azaleas, and white roses, this garden illustrates the harmony and flow of classic design. Shaped hedges of varied heights and carefully contrasted leaf textures lend interest, even where color is not evident. Good brick paths in herringbone patterns give access to secret corners hidden behind evergreens and the twisted, smooth trunks of ancient crape myrtle trees. Built in 1955, the garden perfectly complements the beautiful historic house.

Don't-Miss Feature: Watch for the sundial upheld by cherubs in the central courtyard.

Recognition: The River Oaks Garden Club Forum of Civics Building is listed in the National Register of Historic Places.

Sponsored Activities: Annual Azalea Tour in early spring; annual Environmental Seminar in the winter. Call for information.

Tour Policy: Each year, during two weekends in March, the River Oaks Garden Club sponsors a tour of private and public gardens called the **Azalea Trail.** Proceeds from this affair help to support the club's projects in conservation, horticulture, and civic beautification. The trail includes the Forum building and Bayou Bend Gardens, as well as several private estates in the city and is well worth the small admission charge. (Not all the private sites will be wheelchair accessible.)

The River Oaks Garden Club also offers guided tours of Bayou Bend Collection and Gardens from September through May (see Houston-Bayou Bend).

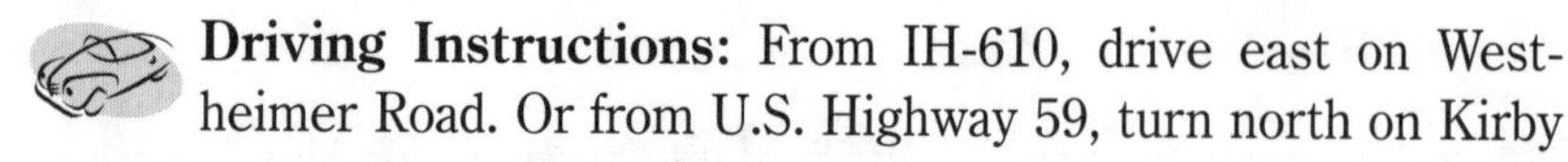

Driving Instructions: From IH-610, drive east on Westheimer Road. Or from U.S. Highway 59, turn north on Kirby

Drive, which will take you to Westheimer. Turn east (right) and look for the site on your right within a block or so.

Houston Garden Center in Hermann Park

Stroud Memorial Rose Garden
Japanese Garden
1500 Hermann Drive
Houston, Texas 77030
713-529-3960; 713-284-1989
http://www.hermannpark.org

Fee: Free.

Accessibility: Excellent.

Days and Hours: 8-8 Monday-Friday; 10-8 Saturday and Sunday. Closed Thanksgiving, Christmas, and New Year's Days.

Garden Type: Public garden.

Garden Size: Several acres. You will enjoy a two-hour stroll.

Themes and Special Features: Rose garden, fragrant garden, Japanese garden. You may also want to visit the Cockrell Butterfly Center in the Museum of Natural Sciences Building in the park. It's in the huge pyramid-shaped building you passed on your left as you entered the park off Montrose.

The Gardens: Spread out around the Houston Garden Center Building, this popular public display is often the setting for weddings, receptions, and other joyous gatherings. More than six million people a year visit the park in which these gardens lie.

Start your tour at the Stroud Memorial Rose Garden, a display garden for the American Rose Society. You will be admiring more than 2,500 specimens of about 100 All-American varieties. They are mostly hybrid tea selections laid out in dedicated beds, creating the classic image of a rose garden. Neatly trimmed grassy paths set off the gently curved ranks of semicircular beds.

Past the rose garden, you will discover beds dedicated to bulbs, camellias, and other perennials. Follow the paths around the grounds until you come to the lovely wooden structure housing the Fragrant Garden. Here you will find raised beds at wheelchair height, filled with luscious herbs of every description. In one bed, mints grow in a profusion of flavors: orange, grapefruit, chocolate, apple, and lemon. In another, scented geraniums waft aloft the aromas of nutmeg, coconut, ginger, chocolate mint, and rose.

When you look up and out from here, skyscrapers loom in every direction. You can hear traffic noise from the heart of one of America's busiest cities. But the effect of this garden is to create and heighten a sense of openness and peace. Maybe the magnificent old trees have something to do with the feeling of tranquility.

Don't-Miss Feature: Take a moment to visit the shade dell, a colorful garden planted where shade from spreading oaks has encroached over once sunny areas. (Never pass up a chance to see a design that works well in shade.)

Very Special Feature: Almost due west across the street and the grounds from the Garden Center lies the five-acre **Japanese Garden**. If you didn't know it was there, you might never locate it, but it's worth the search. Built by renowned Japanese architect Ken Nakajima, it is an outstanding example of Asian art expressed in native Texas materials, including sharp-edged granite boulders where you might traditionally expect nice, round, mossy rocks, and a mix of dogwoods, azaleas, spireas, cherries, and crape myrtles, irises, and grasses quite unlike anything else you're likely to see in Texas, maybe in the world. The tranquility you would expect is here, along with a series of exquisitely designed and built structures, from the gatehouse to the tea garden. Pathways are crushed stone and curved in the traditional manner, with water features, bridges, and stone lanterns adding their own touches of authenticity. The five-piece lantern carved from solid granite and presented as a gift from the city of Chiba, Japan, welcomes visitors as they enter and focuses the spirit of the garden. Throughout the grounds, native pines and oaks lend their own majesty to the scene.

For more information about this very special garden, call 713-284-1914.

Bird Alert: Scissor-tailed flycatcher will be found hunting insects in the park in the summer, joined by yellow-bellied sapsucker, pine siskin, and cedar waxwing in winter.

Sponsored Activities: More than 20 gardening societies meet here regularly, and the building is available for rental. Call 713-284-1986 for details.

Tour and Rental Policy: Tours are self-guided. To inquire about rentals for weddings, reunions, and other get-togethers, call 713-845-1003.

Volunteer and Support Opportunities: The Friends of Hermann Park have big plans for one of Houston's most historic green spaces, and they welcome your interest and aid. Opportunities for one-day service or long-term jobs abound. Charitable gifts they look for include sponsorship of garden furnishings, like benches, tables, and drinking fountains, which can be dedicated as memorials, and contributions to funds for reforesting parkland and restoring and preserving Hermann Park.

Driving Instructions: Hermann Park is located in the southwest region of the city off Main Street, near Rice University, Texas Medical Center, and the Museum District. If you are coming from the north on U.S. Highway 59, take Fannin Street south. Find the second lane from the left and stay in it until you reach the park. If you're coming from the west on U.S. 59, exit at Richmond and follow it east to Fannin and turn right (south). Stay in the second lane from the left until you reach the park. Once there, head toward the huge Sam Houston monument and drive around it. You will pass the Museum of Natural Science and then see the white Garden Center building on your left, with ample parking around it.

Humble-Houston

Mercer Arboretum and Botanic Gardens

22306 Aldine Westfield Road
Humble, Texas 77338-1071
281-443-8731
email: mercerarboretum@cp4.hctx.net
http//www.cp4.hctx.net/mercer

Mercer Arboretum & Botanic Gardens

Fee: Free.

Accessibility: Varies, but very good in many areas, excellent in some. Call ahead if you need special accommodations or a wheelchair.

Days and Hours: During the summer, 8-7 Monday-Saturday; 10-7 Sunday. In winter, closes at 5. There will be something interesting or pretty to look at here every day of the year.

Garden Type: Public arboretum and botanic garden, part of the Harris County Park System.

Garden Size: Two hundred fifty acres.

Themes and Special Features: This is a well-designed, closely maintained park, with both cultivated and natural areas. More than two dozen themes shape the visitor's experience. Just give yourself over to it and let the gardens guide you through. You'll be amazed at the quality of the signage here. Or if you prefer to start with an overview and know right where you're going, you can pick up an excellent map at the Visitor Center.

There are two sections to the park, separated by Aldine Westfield Road. You may wish to start your visit in the eastern section, where the Visitor Center lies. In any case, when you're ready to cross the road to the other section, you'll find a crosswalk on the far north side of the garden. Watch for the signs.

The Gardens: Plant lovers will want to spend the day here. Bring a picnic if you like. You'll find tables set up in the west-side gardens.

Sprawled along both sides of a busy suburban street in the third-largest county in the nation, Mercer Arboretum is an anachronism, a legacy of a time when greenery was more common than concrete and flowers bloomed in the woods beside every stream. A living museum, it showcases extraordinary collections of plants, exhibits a great sense of humor, and maintains its beauty in all seasons.

I like to start a visit here at the east garden, because it lets me go directly to one of my favorite areas, the Salvia Garden. It's introduced by a sign that says, "A rose by any other name…would still be eaten by deer, so we have a salvia garden." If you're a salvia fan, you'll be in heaven here. Mealy cup sage, indigo spires, bog sage, guaranitica, madriensis, elegans, leucantha, glechomifolia, azurea, involucrata—I couldn't name them all. From there, you'll forge your way through the hummingbirds and butterflies past the perennial beds and into the Vine Arbor, where more than 20 different climbing plant species from around the world make themselves at home, twining about the pergolas and trellises, cascading different colors at different seasons, from purple wisteria to white jasmine to red rose.

A Dry Garden features drought-resistant plants; an Endangered Species Garden shows us what scarlet catchfly and Neches River rose mallow look like; a Geophyte Garden collects plants that have underground storage capacities, including lilies and irises of all kinds. Beyond that, you'll find an azalea knot garden, a formal herb garden framed in clipped boxwood, and a daylily garden with its neat rows of varieties all named and tagged. If you follow the sinuous brick path from here through the woods, you'll pass azaleas and flowering perennials under native trees, everything in perfect scale and harmony.

This is a garden that shows intelligent planning in every inch; it's thoroughly civilized without being the least bit stuffy. But if you're ready for more adventure, take the path north toward the crosswalk

and enter another world in the west section, where you will find more naturalized areas devoted to re-creating native habitats from the Big Thicket forest to a prairie wildflower meadow. Here, too, you will find a lovely picnic area with more than fifty tables.

Don't-Miss Feature: It's not shown on the four-color map they hand out, and when the daylilies are in bloom it will be easy to overlook, but just east of the daylily bed, you will find an old-fashioned maze, or labyrinth, created from a dense planting of southern yew. Duck in here. It's a small but intensely satisfying puzzle.

Bird Alert: In winter, look for dark-eyed junco, yellow-bellied sapsucker, and rufous-sided towhee. In spring and summer, you may see various vireos and warblers as well as ruby-throated and black-chinned hummingbirds.

Sponsored Activities: Varied and extensive are the programs, entertainments, children's activities, and learning opportunities here. It seems as if something is going on all the time, and that's year round, from teacher in-service to Master Gardener training and how-to-do-it workshops for homeowners. Scout badges and science projects can get a boost, too. The big plant sale takes place near the end of March every year. You will want to call for a current schedule of events.

Tour and Rental Policies: Tours are self-guided, unless you want to make advance reservations three weeks ahead to have a docent guide your group. They will do it at no charge, but contributions are always appreciated. A big picnic pavilion is available for groups, too. You'll need to get your reservation made for it early, and be prepared to place a deposit (refundable).

Volunteer and Support Opportunities: The Mercer Society is the membership organization that provides philanthropic support for the gardens. Membership, ranging from $25 to $500, gets you access to such goodies as plant-sale discounts and special field trips. But you don't have to belong to this group to volunteer at the Mercer. Just call the volunteer coordinator at 281-443-8731. People of all ages, interests, and skill levels are needed. They will match your talents to their projects and train you in the job if necessary.

Driving Instructions: Mercer is close to Houston International Airport, about 22 miles north of the city itself, in a suburb called Humble. The easiest access is from IH-45. Exit at Farm Road 1960 and drive east. When you reach Aldine Westfield Road, turn north (left). Go a little over a mile and at the second traffic light, turn either right or left into the park grounds. A right turn will take you to the east gardens and the Visitor Center; a left turn takes you into the west section and the picnic grounds. There are parking lots on both sides.

McAllen

McAllen Botanical Gardens and Nature Center

Business U.S. Highway 83 West at Ware Road
P.O. Box 220
McAllen, Texas 78505
956-682-1517

Fee: Free.

Accessibility: Good.

Days and Hours: Open daily during daylight hours.

Garden Type: Nature trail featuring native plants and wildlife.

Garden Size: Twenty acres.

The Gardens: In a county where some 270,000 acres are irrigated to make the most of the 330 growing days each year, public ornamental plantings are somewhat rare. But the McAllen Botanical Garden gives you an opportunity to observe native plants and wildlife, including a cactus garden. You will also find a sunken garden and water features.

Bird Alert: Some of the best birding in the country goes on in this area. Be on the watch for unusual species, especially during spring and fall migrations. Year round, watch for buff-bellied hummingbird, golden-fronted woodpecker, Audubon's oriole, and even pyrrhuloxia.

Tour Policy: Tours are self-guided.

Volunteer and Support Opportunities: The Center is owned and operated by the city of McAllen. Contact Parks and Recreation at the number above for more information.

Driving Instructions: From downtown McAllen, take U.S. Business Highway 83 about 2½ miles west to just past Ware Road on your right.

Quinta Mazatlan

The city of McAllen has recently acquired an historic estate property that encompasses eight acres of gardens and nature trails, as well as an adobe hacienda built in 1935, and is intent on making it into a showplace. Quinta Mazatlan, as it is called, is located at 600 Sunset Avenue in McAllen. More than 150 species of trees, shrubs, vines, and perennials are to be found here, as well as 110 species of birds. The beautiful villa and its grounds will house the McAllen wing of the World Birding Center. If you are in McAllen, this is a not-to-be-missed sight. For more information, contact the Parks and Recreation Department at 956-682-1517 or 956-971-0044.

Nature Lovers Flock to the Valley for Festivals

If you've never seen a chachalaca, a great kiskadee, or an olive sparrow, better show up in late March for the **Texas Tropics Nature Festival** in McAllen. Experts will guide you through the nearby Santa Ana National Wildlife Refuge and point out such treasures, as well as take you on classroom journeys through the cultural and natural history of the region. Butterflies will be migrating through, too, for an extra treat. You can get details and dates from the address below.

Texas Tropics Nature Festival
P.O. Box 790
McAllen, Texas 78505
1-877-McAllen

In November, the communities of Raymondville and Port Mansfield hold a four-day **Nature Odyssey**, celebrating native birds, plants, and butterflies. Call 956-689-3171 for details.

The **Annual Rio Grande Valley Birding Festival** in mid-November presents an opportunity for field trips and workshops by leaders in the birding field. Learn more from the address below.

Harlingen Chamber of Commerce
311 East Tyler
Harlingen, Texas 78550
956-423-5440; 800-531-7346

Butterfly Alert: Don't miss the premier butterfly festival in Texas in the city of Mission.

Texas is home to more recorded species of butterfly than any other state, with more than 400, according to the North American Butterfly Association. Four counties in the Lower Rio Grande account for almost 300 of them.

In Hidalgo County, just west of McAllen, the city of Mission positions itself as the best place in the state to go butterflying any time of year and the only place to be during the third week in October when they hold their Annual Texas Butterfly Festival. Several days of workshops and field trips led by experts, punctuated by visits to the Nature Expo and the Butterfly Conservancy, should satisfy the most insistent appetite to learn about, identify, and even touch one of the state's natural treasures. A parade, a barbecue dinner, and other shenanigans round out the experience. The South Texas Butterfly Club helps the Chamber of Commerce sponsor this event, and if you're spending time in the area and would like to volunteer to work at the festival, give them a call. To learn more, contact:

The Greater Mission Chamber of Commerce
220 E. 9th Street, Mission, Texas 78572
956-585-2727; 800-580-2700
www.texasbutterfly.com

Rockport-Fulton

Annual Hummer/Bird Celebration

Rockport-Fulton Chamber of Commerce
404 Broadway
Rockport, Texas 78382
361-729-6445; 800-242-0071
email: visitor@1rockport.org
http://www.rockport-fulton.org
These plantings are on private property; please treat them accordingly.

Fee: Free for the self-guided tour. Fees are charged for tour buses and seminars.

Accessibility: Variable, but excellent in many locations.

Days and Hours: The celebration is an event held for three weekend days in mid-September every year.

Garden Type: Tours of private gardens, featuring plantings to lure and feed hummingbirds.

Special Features: The event includes programs, speakers, audio-visuals, and vendors, all sharply focused on native plants and wildlife. Very informative sessions, but there will be a fee to attend them.

Rockport and Fulton have joined hands with the local birding clubs to host the festival and to provide tour buses for birding the towns and other area bird sites for a modest fee. Or you can pick up a map at the Chamber and guide yourself on the tour of gardens at private homes.

The Gardens: The towns are full of flowers and the air glitters with birds. The hum, pulse, throb, and whir of wee wings mark the annual return of the ruby-throated hummingbirds, and these Gulf Coast towns throw open the welcome gates and hold a celebration. It's a sight for bird lover and flower lover alike, as citizens invite visitors into private yards to observe the hummers and the blooming plants that feed them.

What are all these hummingbirds doing here in the middle of September? Pausing to feed and refresh themselves and store up energy before embarking on the last leg of their annual migration across the Gulf of Mexico to their summer homes in Mexico and Central America. During their few days here on the coast, they will devour enough nectar and insects to increase their body weight by as much as 50 percent in preparation for the 500-mile nonstop flight. For the past several years, the community has directed considerable effort toward helping them do so, with citizens filling their yards with the kinds of fall-blooming, nectar-filled flowers they feed on. The towns overflow with salvias like Mexican sage, autumn sage, pineapple sage, mealy cup sage, and pitcher sage, as well as morning glory, obedient plant, and turk's cap. Of course, plastic bird feeders abound, too, some having to be filled ten or more times a day at the busiest feeding stations.

Bird Alert: Of the 600 or so bird species that call Texas home for some part of each year, more than 400 show up in this area at one time or another. Most of the hummingbirds are ruby-throated, but you may also spot buff-bellied, black-chinned, and rufous. Year-round residents here include the spectacular crested caracara, green jay, and long-billed thrasher. Shore birds and sea birds are countless, but in September, you should see brown pelicans, roseate spoonbills, and black-bellied whistling duck. Whooping cranes spend the winter nearby.

Volunteer and Support Opportunities: Contact the Chamber of Commerce at the number listed above.

Gift Shop: Vendors will be offering everything from books to jewelry to T-shirts. Food, too.

Driving Instructions: Rockport lies on State Highway 35, about 30 miles northeast of Corpus Christi. Once you get there, watch for signs advising you where to begin your visit.

Chasing the Hummers from East to West

Another famous Texas Hummingbird Festival takes place each year in far West Texas. The **Davis Mountains Hummingbird Festival** beckons bird lovers for three days of seminars, workshops, and field trips in pursuit of up to nine species of hummingbirds that may be found in the area in late summer. You can look for other birds, too, if you like; Fort Davis State Park is full of them, and you can participate in banding activities. For information, contact Prude Ranch at 915-426-3202.

Rockport Demonstration Bird Garden and Wetlands Pond

Rockport-Fulton Chamber of Commerce
404 Broadway
Rockport, Texas 78382
361-729-6445; 800-242-0071
email: visitor@1rockport.org

Fee: Free.

Accessibility: Excellent.

Days and Hours: Open daily.

Garden Type: Native plant garden developed and maintained by the state and community to attract hummingbirds, especially during their fall migration.

Garden Size: Texas Department of Transportation rest stop, with boardwalk and observation platform for birdwatching.

The Garden: As its name implies, this garden demonstrates the value of such natural resources as native plants, wetlands, and birds. The focus is on hummingbirds, thousands of which make their way through the area in the fall, all in search of energy sources to replenish what they've used up getting here and build up stores for the next leg of their flight toward Mexico and Central America. Mid-September is the best time for viewing hummingbirds in hordes.

Bird Alert: Over 400 species of birds occur in this area throughout the year. Most of the hummingbirds are ruby-throated, but you may also spot buff-bellied, black-chinned, and rufous. Year-round residents here include the spectacular crested caracara, green jay, and long-billed thrasher. During the winter watch for whooping crane.

Volunteer and Support Opportunities: Contact the Chamber of Commerce. See numbers above.

Driving Instructions: The rest stop is located north of Rockport on the east side of State Highway 35, about one mile south of the intersection of 35 with Farm Road 3036.

Celebrate the Whooping Cranes

The Rockport/Aransas area is famous for birds on both ends of the size scale—the tiny hummers and the humongous whoopers. The whooping cranes that winter here are literally a national treasure, since they represent about two-thirds of all the birds surviving in the wild.

Their numbers vary from year to year, but every October about 180 whooping cranes soar into Aransas National Wildlife Refuge on the Gulf Coast, 60 miles north of Corpus Christi and very near the villages of Fulton and Rockport. They will feast on blue crabs and clams in the shallow salt marshes until the middle of April, when they will head north again to rear the next generation in Canada's Buffalo National Park, 2,500 miles away.

The whoopers, big enough for even amateur birders to spot, are very popular, and the community likes to recognize their status each year in late winter with a **Celebration of Whooping Cranes and Other Birds**.

Excursions into the bay by boat bring you up close and personal to the birds, at least as close as you are likely ever to get, so don't miss the chance to go out, even if the weather seems dreary. Take your binoculars and camera, and dress in something warm and waterproof. When you get back to shore, dry off and enjoy seminars, art exhibits, and some great seafood. Find out more from the following address.

Port Aransas Chamber of Commerce
421 Cotter
Port Aransas, Texas 78373
800-45-COAST

Victoria

Four Seasons Garden Center

1209 East Salem Road
Victoria, Texas 77904
361-575-8807

Fee: Free.

Accessibility: Excellent.

Days and Hours: 8:30-6 Monday-Saturday; 10-6 Sunday.

Garden Type: Retail nursery with small display garden.

Garden Size: Backyard size.

Themes and Special Features: They grow plumerias from cuttings here. I hope you get to see some in bloom.

The Gardens: This is a retail operation where they understand that what they are selling is not seeds and plants but the future—not a one-gallon plant but a tree. Their beautifully maintained display gardens show what a mature perennial border is supposed to look like, especially one that has been planned to show off contrasting colors and textures. In the store you'll find a sophisticated selection of garden art, high-quality bird feeders, roses, and the annual and perennial plants appropriate to the season.

Driving Instructions: Take U.S. Highway 77 north out of Victoria and turn right onto Salem Road, which is also Farm Road 1315. You will find this pretty little nursery on your right.

Victoria Memorial Rose Garden

Victoria Parks and Recreation Department
P.O. Box 1758
Victoria, Texas 77902
800-926-5774
info@visitvictoria.org

Fee: Free.

Accessibility: Good; be prepared for a bit of a mess after heavy rains, but you can navigate around it if need be.

Days and Hours: Open daily during daylight hours. Best months to visit are April, May, October, and November, but there will be blooms here almost any time you visit, except in the very depths of a harsh winter.

Garden Type: Dedicated rose garden with over 1,000 rose bushes. There is nothing else here.

Garden Size: I wasn't able to determine the exact size of this garden, but I would say about an acre. It is, at any rate, as large as a single-minded garden of this type can be without becoming overwhelming in its feast of riches. The length of time you will want to spend here depends on your taste for lavish feasts.

Themes and Special Features: This is an American Rose Society Display Garden, one of the best I've ever seen.

The Gardens: Everything in this garden is perfect, starting with its setting in a quiet, friendly little city's family-oriented park, where, when you step out of your car and close the door, the sound startles the northern mockingbird out of the tree by the gate, and then the only sounds are the far-off call of a dove and the gurgle of a water feature just inside the white metal fence in front of you. Oh, and if you listen a moment, you may catch the gentle snick of a keeper's clippers as she manicures her charges, the ranks of roses set out in semicircular raised beds, edged in no-nonsense concrete, and traversed by smooth pea gravel paths. Inside the garden, a shaded bench beckons visitors to catch their breath before venturing out into a sea of roses, most of them modern hybrid teas, but shrubs and climbers and grandifloras are included, as well, all planted as memorials, "In loving memory of..." someone whose memory is worthy of having a rose bush dedicated to it.

I've never seen such roses as I saw here one bright November morning—huge, luscious blooms on bushes glowing with health, filling the air with perfume. Every color imaginable, every size, shape, and fragrance make this a rose lover's paradise.

Don't-Miss Feature: If you sit on the bench beneath the tree near the gate, you may be pelted by a spiky-looking ball moss that sometimes falls like ripe fruit.

Bird Alert: Right on the Guadalupe River, some 35 miles from the Gulf of Mexico, with woods and wildlands on all sides, Riverside Park is home to scores of bird species all year long. Among the pecan and cedar elm trees in the park you can spot a summer tanager or eastern bluebird in summer, winter wren, pine warbler, or fox sparrow in winter. If you happen to look up at the right time, you could even see whooping cranes.

Part of the Central Texas Coastal Birding Trail, the park is especially valuable for its spring and fall migrations. Well over 250 bird species have been sighted within 50 miles of the city of Victoria.

Tour Policy: Tours are self-guided.

Volunteer and Support Opportunities: Call Parks and Recreation at 361-572-2767.

Driving Instructions: To find the Rose Garden, you must first find Riverside Park. That means finding U.S. Highway 87 north of Rio Grande Street. Highway 87 is also Main Street. From it you will turn west on Magnolia Avenue and drive into the park. Playing fields line both sides of the road as you follow its curves. Watch on the left for the white metal fence of the rose garden or signs for the Parks and Recreation Office. Turn left into the parking lot, turn off the ignition, open a door, and sit silently for a moment enjoying the tranquility.

"Mankind and roses seem to be eternally linked, especially in the South, where climate and soils encourage a flowering of so many types."

William C. Welch and Greg Grant, *The Southern Heirloom Garden*

Weslaco

Valley Nature Center

301 South Border
Weslaco, Texas 78599
956-969-2475
http://www.valleynaturecenter.org

Fee: Adults $2; Children $1.

Accessibility: Good.

Days and Hours: Tuesday-Friday 9-5; Saturday 8-5; Sunday 1-5.

Garden Type: Educational nature park featuring native flora unique to the local ecosystem. They call this "a secret garden in the heart of the Rio Grande Valley."

Garden Size: Five acres.

Themes and Special Features: Since natural habitat is carefully maintained, you may catch sight of a Texas tortoise or horned lizard.

The Gardens: Nicely labeled exhibits laid out along short hiking trails offer access to sample vegetation from several diverse areas, from the Sabal Palm Grove to the Chihuahuan Thorn Forest. Don't miss the Cactus Garden, the Bog Garden, and the Butterfly Garden, which provides fantastic butterfly viewing all year long. The species you could encounter in different seasons are too numerous even to begin listing here, but Mexican bluewing, pale-banded crescent, Julia, and violet-banded skipper are among them. Be sure to pick up a seasonal checklist.

Bird Alert: Birds are your constant companions as you tour these grounds. A few of the species recorded by the Center staff as year-round residents include plain chachalaca, green parakeet, red-crowned parrot, great kiskadee, white-eyed vireo, and Audubon's oriole. Buff-bellied hummingbird may be hanging around in the summer.

Sponsored Activities: Dedicated to educating its constituency in the beauty and value of their native plants and animals, the Center presents a full slate of programs for both school children and adults. They sponsor field trips for birders and summer nature camps for children and keep a full complement of volunteers busy.

Gift Shop: The shop offers an excellent selection of field guides to birds, bats, butterflies, and other critters, and other books about Texas and its fauna and flora.

Tour Policy: Tours are self-guided.

Volunteer and Support Opportunities: Memberships in the sponsoring organization range from $10 for a Winter Texan up to $1,000 for a lifetime commitment, with plenty of reasonably priced choices between. As a member, you'll get a monthly newsletter, free admission to the Center and its programs, and your choice of jobs, from greeting visitors to weeding the garden.

Driving Instructions: From U.S. Business Highway 83 in Weslaco, turn south on Border Street. Go one block to Gibson Park.

Finding More Flowers in South Texas

Brownsville

Visit the Gladys Porter Zoo and enjoy tropical and semitropical plants in bloom as you explore the animal exhibits. Located at 300 Ringgold Street, it's open all day, every day. The small admission is well spent. The number is 956-546-7187.

Houston

The Lone Star Koi Club annually sponsors an elaborate tour of ponds and water gardens on private property, usually in June. You can pick up information and verify this year's dates at any nursery in the Houston area that sells water gardening products, and that's most of them.

Daylily Display Gardens

You will find American Hemerocallis Society Daylily Display Gardens at private homes in several communities in this region. They will open to the public during specific dates in the late spring and early summer. Call for details.

Alvin
Harvey and Nell Shimek, 281-331-4395

Pearland
Leon and Paula Payne, 281-485-3821

Waller
Leon and Martha Overby, 936-372-5729

Part Six

The Gardens of West Texas

Alpine, Amarillo, Del Rio, El Paso, Hale Center, Fort Davis, Lajitas-Terlingua, Lubbock, Mineral Wells, San Angelo

"Rocks Rule in West Texas."

Janet Edwards, Travel Writer

Rocks do indeed hold court in far West Texas, where volcanic eruptions and mountain uplifts shaped the land millions of years ago. But throughout much of the stretch of endless miles we call West Texas, an outcropping of rocks would be a welcome break in the flat, featureless landscape.

We're talking flat. So flat in some parts that early settlers didn't dare start across the plains without a compass tied to the saddlehorn.

Lots of people glory in it, including relatives of mine—the endless reaches of sky and road—a horizon always in view, no matter where you are. In fact, when I first encountered forests as a young child, I didn't know the word for it, but what I experienced was a mild form of claustrophobia. Everywhere I looked there were trees. Where was the horizon!

Now, of course, I've learned to value compromise. I like rolling plains and being able to find where I am on the planet, but not to the utter foreswearing of trees, shrubs, and flowers. That's why I don't live in this area any more. The relatives can't imagine wanting to live anywhere else.

And when I visit them in spring or early summer, I almost remember why. Wildflowers along the interstate highways, for one thing. What a treasure the Texas Department of Transportation has created, planting native and adapted flowering species that not only provide erosion control and wildlife habitat, but produce a splendid canvas of color along the roadside, as well. In the westernmost reaches, cacti spring into bloom after a rain. In the Panhandle, sunflowers raised as cash crops in irrigated fields follow the sun's daily path with cheerful faces, and cotton turns fields white in the fall.

And it's not really all totally flat. Today impossibly tall grain elevators stand reaching toward the skies in the midst of Panhandle fields turned rich through irrigation. Oil derricks and nodding pumps mark horizons, too. And towns thrive in the shade the settlers brought with them and planted there, while in the west, mountains rise, some of them to over 8,000 feet.

North to south, east to west, this is a region of enormous variation. Gently rolling hills, grassy savannas, pecan orchards, cotton fields, truck farms, pastureland, woodlands, prairies, mountains, and deserts can all be found here.

And cactus. More species of cactus than in all the other states combined, some of them rare or endangered or found growing nowhere else on earth.

What ties all this diversity together into one vast region is water, or lack of it. Rainfall ranges from some twenty inches a year around San Angelo to less than eight inches near El Paso. And while irrigation assures several western counties a place among state leaders in farm income, much of what the traveler's eye will take in will seem the antithesis of the cultivated public garden.

Strangely enough, some of the state's most interesting or significant gardens are found in this arid region. The people who live here do not take the blessings of shade tree and flower for granted. Where plants are cultivated, they are cared for with pride and diligence. In plantings where natives hold sway, individual specimens tend to be carefully labeled and laid out to display their best features and uses. Where cultivated gardens are not feasible, nature trails take their place, especially in public parks like Fort Jackson or Fort Stockton State Historical Parks and at Lubbock's Lake Landmark.

This area also holds some of the most tourist-worthy real estate in Texas. Visitors from all over the world come here seeking the landscape made famous in Hollywood movies about the Old West. What they find here and revel in includes Big Bend National Park, the Chisos and Davis Mountain ranges, the Chihuahuan Desert, historic sites, many restored or well preserved, a world-class observatory that welcomes visitors and puts on a great show for them, raft trips down the Rio Grande, hiking, birding, and wildlife viewing, and museums galore.

And plants, somehow, are a part of all of this. In San Angelo you will find a source of municipal pride in an internationally recognized water lily garden. In El Paso and Lubbock, rose gardens flourish. Hale Center celebrates cacti. Alpine, El Paso, Fort Davis, and Lajitas pay homage to the beauty and toughness of regional natives both in the cultivated landscape and in the wild.

On the far eastern edge of this region, where rainfall nears thirty inches a year, lies a garden young yet but spectacular and destined, I believe, to become a major botanic site for the state—Clark Gardens in Mineral Wells.

As for birds, who would guess that Fort Davis is one of the hummingbird capitals of the world? As many as nine species of hummingbirds can be seen here if you're looking at the right time of the year, especially during late summer migrations. A Hummingbird Festival marks that occasion, with a few days set aside each year to hear experts lecture and to follow guides in hopes of capturing a glimpse of a once-in-a-lifetime bird.

Birdlife diversifies, like the plants, depending on which part of the region you're visiting. In the northern reaches, look for ring-necked pheasant and ferruginous hawk. Sandhill cranes winter at Muleshoe National Wildlife Refuge, northwest of Lubbock. As for the Big Bend area, serious birders can devote a lifetime to the study of bird species there, with Lucifer hummingbird heading the list.

A word to the wise birder. In parts of this area, you will need to switch your field guide from the "Birds of the East" version, which you use throughout much of the state, to the "Birds of the West" version. Otherwise, a lot of birds are going to end up noted simply as LBJs (little brown jobbies) in your field notes.

"...the driest year on record in Texas. That 'honor' goes to 1917, when the entire state's total annual rainfall was just 14.3 inches."

Sherrie S. McLeroy, *First in the Lone Star State*

Threatened or Endangered Texas Cacti

Because of habitat reduction or unbridled collection from the wild, at least nine species of Texas cactus are being driven to extinction and as such are protected under both state and federal laws. Texas Parks and Wildlife Department lists them on its web site: http://www.tpwd.state.tx.us.nature/endang/plants/index.

"They [cacti] are as American as corn, tomatoes, tobacco, or potatoes."

Del Weniger, *Cacti of the Southwest*

Alpine

Sul Ross State University Cactus Garden

Department of Biology
Sul Ross State University
Box C-64
Alpine, Texas 79832
915-837-8112
email: museum@sulross.edu
http://www.sulross.edu/content.asp?ID=150

Fee: Free.

Accessibility: Good.

Days and Hours: Open daily during daylight hours.

Garden Type: An educational display garden featuring cacti from the northern Chihuahuan Desert.

Garden Size: Four 20' by 80' sections, plus several smaller ones.

The Gardens: What you will find here are about 124 kinds of cacti indigenous to the northern Chihuahuan Desert, as well as other true desert plants. This collection is part of the Museum of the Big Bend housed in Lawrence Hall and forms a focal point for the main entry to that building.

Bird Alert: Keep your eyes open. Some pretty colorful birds find themselves on this campus from time to time. Vermilion flycatcher, any of the three bluebirds, painted bunting, and blue grosbeak may show up. Hawks overhead could be any of several species, including rough-legged and Harris's.

Tour Policy: Tours are self-guided unless you can catch a hapless biology student puttering around in the beds and sweet talk yourself a short lecture on the plantings.

Driving Instructions: The gardens are located in front of Lawrence Hall at the entrance to the Sul Ross campus. Take State Highway 90 to the campus.

Amarillo

Amarillo Botanical Gardens

AMARILLO BOTANICAL GARDENS

1400 Streit Drive
Amarillo, Texas 79106
806-352-6513
email: jackie@amarillobotanicalgardens.org
http://www.amarillobotanicalgardens.org

Fee: Free.

Accessibility: Good.

 **Days and Hours:** Open 10-5 Tuesday-Friday, 1-5 Saturday and Sunday.

Garden Type: This is a garden designed to provide horticultural education for the region. It includes display gardens, a conservatory, a gallery for exhibitions, classrooms, and a 1,600-volume library, making it a valuable resource for the community.

Garden Size: Four acres.

Themes and Special Features: A water catchment system helps teach water conservation, while demonstration plantings display successful plants for the High Plains. There's also a touch-and-smell sensory garden.

The Gardens: Herbs, flowering perennials and annuals, water plants, and water features make this a pleasurable oasis on the West Texas Plains. The Kate Graham Daylily Garden performs its magic in late spring.

Photo courtesy Amarillo Botanical Gardens

Don't-Miss Feature: Visit the nearby Don Harrington Discovery Center for hands-on science activities for all ages, aquariums for both freshwater and saltwater fish, and a Foucault pendulum.

Bird Alert: Amarillo is a very urbanized area, but if you look up into summer skies, you may well spot one of the Mississippi kites that nest in the area gliding over the roofs and snatching insect prey from the air. Closer to the ground watch for blue jay and American robin.

Sponsored Activities: With a full spectrum of classes, activities, and projects, this botanical garden fulfills its mission to educate the public in the joys of horticulture. Call for a current schedule.

Volunteer and Support Opportunities: Volunteers are absolutely key to the success and expansion of the garden. The Hortus Guild focuses and funnels volunteer activities, including leading tours and doing hands-on gardening. You can reach them at the number above. Amarillo Botanical Gardens is a nonprofit organization and welcomes memberships and donations.

Driving Instructions: If you can find Route 66, you can find the Harrington Regional Medical Center. Turn north from Route 66 into the complex. The garden lies on Streit between Hagy Boulevard and Killgore Drive.

Del Rio

Whitehead Memorial Museum

1308 South Main Street
Del Rio, Texas 78840
830-774-7568
email: inquire@whitehead-museum.com
http://www.whitehead-museum.com

Fee: Adults $4; Seniors $3; Teenagers $2; Children 6-12 $1.

Accessibility: Good.

Days and Hours: 9-4:30 Tuesday-Saturday; 1-5 Sunday; closed Monday.

Garden Type: Landscaped grounds for historical museum.

Garden Size: The entire site covers two and a half acres.

Themes and Special Features: This is an open-air museum, with 20 exhibits ranging from a replica of Judge Roy Bean's Jersey Lilly Saloon to a living prairie dog domicile.

Photo courtesy Whitehead Memorial Museum

The Gardens: The plantings feature expanses of cool lawn and shade from well-tended trees. Colorful flowers appear in season. A popular place for weddings and receptions, this modest garden is an oasis of freshness just when you need one the most.

Don't-Miss Feature: Kids will love the railroad caboose, as well as the log cabin and blacksmith shop. A collection of barbed wire and another of Indian artifacts are also eyecatching.

Bird Alert: Canyon wren, white-throated swift, cliff swallow, and barn swallow may be found in the neighborhood. The hawk soaring overhead is more likely to be a red-tailed than the rare zone-tailed, but who knows? Train your binocs on it just in case. Mourning dove and northern mockingbird live here, too.

Sponsored Activities: Since the theme here is Texas history, most of the events and activities center around historical topics. Special events are usually planned for major holidays. Call to find out about scheduled events, because the folks here like to have fun. Something is sure to be going on.

Tours and Rental Policies: Weddings, receptions, business and club meetings, and other gatherings can be accommodated here. They can cater a simple meal or set up a wedding complete with everything from chairs to candelabras to packets of birdseed to throw at the happy couple. Call with plenty of advance notice.

Volunteer and Support Opportunities: Museums always need volunteers and contributors. If Texas history and its preservation interest you, this museum epitomizing much of what we think of as "life on the frontier" is well worth looking into.

Driving Instructions: Just drive south on Main Street.

El Paso

Chihuahuan Desert Gardens of the Centennial Museum at the University of Texas at El Paso

Centennial Museum
University of Texas at El Paso
El Paso, Texas 79968-0533
915-747-5565
email: museum@mail.utep.edu
http://www.utep.edu/museum/home.html

Fee: Free.

Accessibility: Good.

Days and Hours: Open during daylight hours.

Garden Type: A teaching and research garden open to the public for both formal and informal education in the use of native plants in the low-water landscape. Dedicated to the flora and the region, this assemblage of 430 species is one of the largest collections of Chihuahuan Desert plants in the world.

Garden Size: Two acres.

Themes and Special Features: Indigenous plants suitable for desert landscaping.

The Gardens: The hardscape in these gardens contributes as much as do the plants. Paths, raised beds, and edgings, all of natural stone and other suitable materials, are a hallmark of this remarkable layout.

Divided into more than two dozen gardens of varying sizes and themes by low stone walls and other features, the plantings accentuate the beauty of the Centennial Museum Building.

When you leave your car in the Museum parking lot, a barrel cactus points the way to the Desert Shrub Garden, a collage of pungent-smelling native shrubs, like creosote bush and turpentine bush. Paths also lead you through the Succulent Garden, with its somewhat more familiar agaves and yuccas, to something you really didn't expect to find—a tiny Contemplative Garden featuring colorful flowers around a distinctive drip fountain.

Further on, the Terrace Garden showcases plants from the Eastern Chihuahuan Desert. A charming amphitheater anchors a kind of courtyard where, after a rain, Texas sage bursts into lavender bloom, along with six other Leucophyllum species.

Keep exploring. You will find in quick succession a Wall Garden, an Arroyo Garden, a Grass Garden, and many others, including a most welcome sanctuary for butterflies, hummingbirds, and humans, a Sensory Garden. Here, sweet Mexican marigold, chocolate daisy, Mexican oregano, and other fragrant herbs soften the air.

Even a water garden looks right in this setting, complete with a catch basin and a seep spring. They've designed it with huge boulders and plantings of native grasses and frog fruit, a scene that is both inviting and natural looking.

Bird Alert: White-winged dove is here year round. In winter you will also find dark-eyed junco and perhaps lesser goldfinch. Broad-billed hummingbirds are a summer treat.

Sponsored Activities: The Centennial Museum has a mission to educate the public about the cultural and natural history of the region. To that end, their schedule is full of workshops for students and teachers, as well as outreach programs for the schools.

Tour Policy: Tours are self-guided, but signage is adequate.

Driving Instructions: You will find the Centennial Museum on the UTEP campus west of downtown at the intersection of University Avenue and Wiggins Way. You can take IH-20 west to the exit for Shuster and follow the signs.

El Paso Municipal Rose Garden

1702 North Copia
El Paso, Texas 79930
915-541-4331

El Paso Parks & Recreation
THE ROSE GARDEN

Fee: Free.

Accessibility: Good.

Days and Hours: Open March through October, 8-3 Tuesday-Friday, 8-noon Saturday.

Garden Type: Dedicated rose garden; All-American Selection Rose Garden.

Garden Size: About 1,500 plants of nearly 200 varieties.

The Gardens: This is a very pretty garden in a dramatic landscape. Mountains in the backdrop and brilliant desert sun remind the visitor that this is not what one normally thinks of as rose country. But with irrigation, the shrubs and climbers thrive in their fertile raised beds, exalting in the arid air that leaves them free of black spot and other disfiguring fungi. Low stone walls and comfortable paths complete the image of a well-loved and maintained municipal garden. April and May present a glorious show, with October close behind.

Bird Alert: This garden lies in the heart of urban El Paso, the fourth largest city in Texas, but Memorial Park is home to many birds, including those adapted to life in town, like great-tailed grackle. The hummingbird you see will probably be a black-chinned, but broad-tailed, calliope, or rufous can show up, too. Golden-crowned kinglet flits through the pines in winter, and several kinds of flycatchers chase insects all summer long.

Sponsored Activities: Rose planting and pruning demonstrations are given each year by the El Paso Rose Society, along with spring and fall Open Garden events. Call 915-598-4970 or 915-751-3631 to learn about scheduled events.

Tour and Rental Policies: You can get all your questions about roses answered at one of the twice-a-year Open Gardens. Call the number above for dates and times.

And you can rent this lovely site for a wedding, reception, or other event at quite reasonable rates. Call 915-598-0771.

Volunteer and Support Opportunities: The City Parks and Recreation Department depends heavily on members of the Rose Society to keep the garden looking its best. If you want to pitch in, call 915-598-4970 or 915-751-3631.

Driving Instructions: The rose garden sits at the intersection of North Copia and Aurora at the northeast end of Memorial Park. From IH-10, take Piedras Street north and turn right (east) on Pershing Drive, then left on Copia.

Texas A&M Agricultural Research and Extension Center

Xeriscape Demonstration Display Garden
Texas A&M University
1380 A&M Circle
El Paso, Texas 79927
email: a-michelsen@tamu.edu
http://elpaso.tamu.edu/Research/Index.htm

Fee: Free.

Accessibility: Good during the week. Gates may be closed on weekends.

Days and Hours: Open daily during daylight hours.

Garden Type: Demonstration xeriscape garden, using plants native to the Chihuahuan Desert, as well as other arid regions, for research and education.

Themes and Special Features: Dry can be beautiful. This carefully groomed landscaping display garden proves it.

The Gardens: Designed to show homeowners acceptable alternatives to green lawns and high-water-usage trees and shrubs, the garden showcases such beauties as cholla in purple bloom or bearing yellow fruit, goldball leadtree, rock cotoneaster, sotol, opuntia, and other colorful species. Placed in neat and weed-free raised or edged beds, mulched with organic materials from pecan shells to Christmas tree trimmings, plants boast legible signs, so you will know what you're looking at. Orderly paths made of changing surface materials lend interest. If you live in a region where low-water plants are gaining popularity, or if xeriscaping appeals to you as a homeowner, bring a notebook and pen so you can jot down some of the innovative ideas you'll find here.

Bird Alert: There's an Audubon Society Sanctuary nearby with a small lake that hosts various herons and egrets and sometimes a migrating white-faced ibis or wintering tundra swan. Both rock dove and mourning dove are common, as are black-chinned hummingbird and killdeer. No telling what you'll see flying over if you look up.

Tour Policy: Tours are self-guided. Excellent signage makes the trip a pleasure and an education.

Driving Instructions: The TAMU campus is located east of El Paso. From El Paso, take IH-10 to Exit 34 and stay on the access road (Gateway West) under Americas Avenue. Bear to the right at the cloverleaf toward Americas Avenue South. Cross the bridge and immediately head for the exit for IH-10 East toward Van Horn. That will put you on Gateway East. Look for the green sign at A&M Circle that says "Texas A&M Research Center." Turn right and the Center will be on your left.

Fort Davis

Chihuahuan Desert Research Institute and Visitor Center

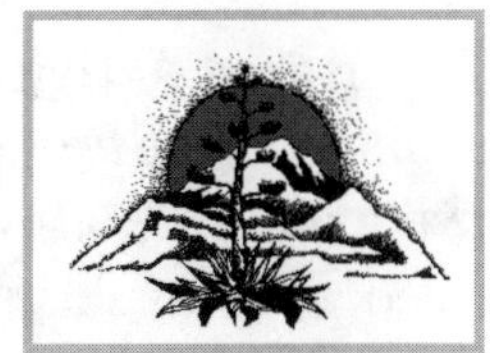

P.O. Box 905
Fort Davis, Texas 79734
(see Driving Instructions below)
915-364-2499
email: manager@cdri.org
http://www.cdri.org

Fee: Small admission fee charged.

Accessibility: Varies, but is pretty limited.

Days and Hours: Open 9-5 Monday-Friday. Open 9-5 Saturday April 1 through Labor Day. Closed Thanksgiving and Christmas Days.

Garden Type: Well-marked nature trail; arboretum, greenhouses, gift shop, landscaping displays.

Garden Size: The Center sits on a 507-acre site. The arboretum covers about 20 acres. The hiking trail is about a half-mile round trip.

Themes and Special Features: The greenhouse brings together one of the largest collections of live Chihuahuan Desert cacti and succulents there is on public display anywhere.

The Gardens: The Visitors' Center is beautifully landscaped with native plants, including grasses, sages, cacti, and shrubs.

Don't-Miss Feature: If you're up to a moderately difficult hike, go down the Modesta Canyon Trail to the hidden springs at the mouth of the canyon. Depending on the season, you will be rewarded by mountain laurel, scarlet bouvardia, or Mexican buckeye in bloom along the slopes, or maybe cardinal flower or trumpet flower and some of the many cacti and succulents along the way.

Bird Alert: You may want to pick up a birding checklist in the gift shop before starting out. There are some great birds here, including phainopepla, greater roadrunner, acorn woodpecker, and four species of wrens, each one noisier than the last.

Sponsored Activities: Seminars and lectures go on throughout the summer, some free, some with a small admission. The big Native Plant Sale comes the last week in April, when many species of trees, shrubs, cacti, and succulents will be available for purchase. Call for this year's date.

Tour Policy: Tours are self-guided. Guided tours can be arranged for groups.

Gift Shop: Nature in all its glory is the theme here, with emphasis on learning to appreciate it, care for it, and live wisely in it.

Volunteer and Support Opportunities: You can make a donation to the institute itself or to the Chihuahuan Desert Foundation. Memberships in the Research Institute are an important source of funding and bring with them discounts for lectures, first choice at the plant sale, and other nice benefits. Memberships start at $15 for students and range all the way to $1,000 for Individual Lifetime, but most families will find the $35 family membership quite affordable.

Driving Instructions: The Institute is on State Highway 118, about four miles south of the town of Fort Davis.

Hotel Limpia Herb Garden

P.O. Box 1341
Fort Davis, Texas 79734 (see Driving Instructions below)
800-662-5517
email: frontdesk@hotellimpia.com
http://www.hotellimpia.com

Fee: Free.

Accessibility: Good.

Days and Hours: Open daily during daylight hours.

Garden Type: Herb garden with old roses; a display garden for Hotel Limpia.

Garden Size: Backyard sized.

Themes and Special Features: Gorgeous herbs! This must be where herb plants go to get their wings after we kill them in our heavy, wet soil in North and East Texas. Gardeners, here is rosemary to die for, lavender you won't believe till you smell it. Mints, too, of course, oregano, and all the festive little ornaments you'd expect in a garden that's obviously someone's pride and joy, including, last time I was here, a fat yellow cat.

Bird Alert: Blue-throated, broad-tailed, and black-chinned hummingbirds are all known to hang out here occasionally, along with about six others. This area is one of the hummingbird meccas of Texas.

Gift Shop: This gift store is a souvenir shopper's dream house. You'll find everything here from books about fat cats (like the one in the garden) to herb-scented candles, cards, fancy dinnerware, and home accessories. The nature store, called Javelinas and Hollyhocks, is just a hop across the street.

Tour Policy: Tours are self-guided. Just be sure to allow yourself time to sit and smell the herbs.

You may also want to look over the old hotel. It's a smashing place to spend a night or two, though reservations will be necessary during the summer months.

Driving Instructions: The hotel is located downtown on Main Street, across from the courthouse. The garden is in a courtyard in back, but you don't have to go through the hotel to get to it. Enter from the side street near the hotel gift shop.

Hummingbirds in the Desert

Fort Davis is the headquarters for the annual **Davis Mountains Hummingbird Festival**, which lures bird lovers into the area for three days of seminars and workshops in late summer every year. The highlight of the event for most folks is the chance to take a field trip with an experienced guide in search of some of the nine species of hummingbirds that may be found here. You can look for other birds, too, and participate in banding activities. For information, contact Prude Ranch at 915-426-3202 or prude@overland.net.

Hale Center

Bell Park Cacti Garden

Avenue K
Hale Center, Texas 79041
806-839-2642

Fee: Free.

Accessibility: Good.

Days and Hours: Open daily during daylight hours.

Garden Type: Dedicated to cacti.

Garden Size: About half an acre.

The Gardens: Some 350 plants of dozens of cactus varieties line a winding path through this vista of dryland natives. The same soil, when irrigated, yields big crops of cotton, soy, and grains, making Hale County a major producer of food crops. Dry, it's perfect for cacti.

Bird Alert: Watch for greater roadrunner and ferruginous hawk.

Driving Instructions: Hale Center lies southwest of Plainview. Take the Hale Center exit from State Highway 27 and go west. You will find Bell's at the intersection of Avenue K and Cleveland Street.

Lajitas-Terlingua

Barton Warnock Environmental Education Center

HC 70, Box 375
Terlingua, Texas 79852
915-424-3327
http://www.tpwd.state.tx.us/park/barton

Fee: Free.

Accessibility: Good in buildings.

Days and Hours: Open daily 8-4:30.

Garden Type: Botanical garden featuring plants native to the Chihuahuan Desert. Interpretive Center for the study of local history and natural history.

Garden Size: Two-acre botanical garden set within 99.9 acres of natural area.

Themes and Special Features: Average rainfall here is a whisker under nine inches. Expect to get an education in the wonders of desert existence.

The Gardens: This state park is where you stop to get your bearings and take a big breath before you enter Big Bend Ranch State Park from the east. The Interpretive Center houses exhibits focusing on the geology, archeology, and botany of the area. The bookstore is a treasure house of information about the natural wonders you see around you, from rattlesnakes to mountain peaks.

This is also where you get permits and pay user fees to go into the park.

Tour the garden to see hedgehog, prickly pear, and other cacti, as well as assorted non-cacti, like Texas wolfberry, gumdrop tree, and bird of paradise.

Don't-Miss Feature: The center houses one of the niftiest painted murals you'll ever encounter, featuring a very realistic-looking Tyrannosaurus rex.

Bird Alert: The biological diversity here echoes the habitat diversity, with about 400 bird species having been identified in the Big Bend area. Some of the rarer birds you may catch a glimpse of nearby include Lucifer hummingbird, varied bunting, elf owl, and Chrissal thrasher.

Sponsored Activities: Special events and classes are held in the newly renovated auditorium.

Gift Shop: The store features a selection of appropriately touristy T-shirts and caps, as well as stationery, souvenirs, and educational toys and books.

Tour Policy: Tours of both building and garden are self-guided, unless you want to make arrangements for a group tour by calling ahead.

Driving Instructions: If you're in Lajitas, just take Farm Road 170 east one mile. Or, from Alpine, take State Highway 118 south 78 miles to Study Butte and turn west on Farm Road 170. Stay on it till you get there.

Lubbock

Lubbock Memorial Arboretum

Clapp Park
4111 University Avenue
Lubbock, Texas 79413
806-797-4520
email:
lubarbo@lubbockarboretum.org
http://www.lubbockarboretum.org

Fee: Free.

Accessibility: Good.

Days and Hours: Garden open daily during daylight hours.

Garden Type: Arboretum and research site, exhibiting landscape use of native and adapted plants.

Garden Size: Fifty-five acres.

Themes and Special Features: Rose Garden, Green and White Garden, Fragrance Garden, Japanese Garden, historic Episcopal church building; a center for educational programs.

The Gardens: This garden shows what determination can create—if it has enough water. One hundred fifty varieties of roses find a well-irrigated and maintained home here. You'll enjoy a native plant area here, too, and those towering treasures, oak, pecan, and hackberry trees, offering shade to the weary. Resting spots take regular advantage of the shade throughout the garden. Paths are wide and comfortable. Signs abound. Anytime except winter, which comes earlier here than in most of the state, you will want to relax awhile in this quietly colorful spot, especially if you've been wandering around West Texas very long.

Bird Alert: The Llano Estacado Chapter of the National Audubon Society reports that almost 300 bird species put in a regular appearance in this part of the country, including ten kinds of hawks and three kinds of eagles. In the park, you may find golden-fronted woodpecker and such urbanized birds as blue jay and great-tailed grackle, plus ducks and geese during winter months. If you venture out into the wooded areas during spring and fall migration times, you're going to need a bird identification book. About 30 sparrows have been recorded in their seasons, as well as two dozen different warblers.

Sponsored Activities: On the second Saturday of every month, folks come to the Center to learn more about what they can grow in their own region, what trees, roses, vegetables, and flowers to plant and how to care for them. These hour-long sessions are free and are conducted by professionals and educators, people who have something valuable to offer.

Other popular events include an Arboretum-coordinated Tour of Home Gardens each spring and a similar Tour of Water Gardens in late summer. Call for a current schedule.

Tour Policy: Tours are self-guided, unless you have a crowd that needs some help. To arrange for a docent to conduct your group through the arboretum, call 806-797-4520.

Volunteer and Support Opportunities: The city of Lubbock takes care of utilities and general maintenance and lends a hand with planting when needed, but the day-to-day planting, pruning, weeding, and other chores fall to a very able volunteer corps. They welcome visitors, guide tours, hold workshops, and get their hands in the dirt. They will find some way for you to contribute if you want to get involved. Donations, memorials, and honoraria are always welcome, of course, and memberships are available.

Driving Instructions: From IH-27 on the south side of town, follow the signs to reach the Texas Tech campus. University Avenue runs along the east side of the campus. Take it south to 41st

Street. Or, from Loop 289, take the University exit and go north about two miles. Don't worry, you'll recognize the park when you get to it. Keep going until you see the Arboretum sign.

Mineral Wells

Clark Gardens

567 Maddux Road
P.O. Box 276
Mineral Wells, Texas 76068
940-682-4856
email: info@clarkgardens.com
http://www.clarkgardens.com

Fee: Adults $6; Seniors and Children $4. Pick up a map and hang on to it.

Accessibility: Good.

Days and Hours: Open daily from early April through June and then again in the fall; times may vary from one year to another, so if you're planning to travel very far to get here, call or check the web site to make sure the gardens will be open.

Garden Type: Privately owned botanical garden, one of the most extensive in the state.

Garden Size: When complete, about 50 gardens will cover more than 80 acres. Be warned—there is so much to see here that one day may not afford enough time. April through June and September through November are the best seasons, but even in the summer, canna lilies, crape myrtles, zinnias, and other heat-tolerant annuals and ornamental grasses keep interest high. By the middle of September, roses are gearing up again for their big fall show.

Themes and Special Features: The designers of this estate-type garden were obviously inspired by the estate gardens of England and Europe. Their challenge is to translate that vision into a reality on the dry prairie land of West Texas. Their success speaks for itself in the use of native and adapted trees, shrubs, and flowering plants to create one of the premier gardens in the state of Texas.

The Gardens: Part of the fun of this lush place is finding it in its very Texas setting. You drive down a narrow country lane, through mesquite scrub, junipers, and scraggly late-season wildflowers, up a rise that passes for a hill hereabouts, wondering what dinky little marvel will be revealed when you reach your goal. The last sight you expect is a regal stone entryway, black swans floating on mirrored water, whole gardens turned over to the cultivation of roses, herbs, daylilies, shade-loving flowers, azaleas.

And trees. Magnificent mature specimens of blue atlas cedar, bald cypress, river birch, red oak, Mexican buckeye, willow oak, and post oak. Wide graveled paths through seas of color: azalea, columbine, coralberry, hydrangea, and peony in the shade garden. Blue mistflower, complete with its contingent of feeding butterflies, lantana, Texas sage, and other hardy natives in sunny brick beds. Mass plantings of iris, cannas, and lilies. Gardens devoted to salvias, coneflowers, mallows. Two rose gardens. Woodland and wetland trails. A Children's Garden. Fountains, spouting heads on walls, minuscule lily ponds, streams, statuary, bridges, lakes, waterfalls....

Don't-Miss Feature: Sometimes, you will find plants for sale here. On one visit I found garden-grown trees in one-gallon pots, Texas madrone, vasey oak, smooth mountain mahogany, and Bigelow oak, and thinnings from the perennial beds, including daylilies and coneflower. In early June they sell rose cuttings, and in October they host a Plant Fair. Look for such offerings where the grove of native oaks and junipers beckons you toward picnic tables before you even buy your ticket to go into the garden.

Bird Alert: Trees here harbor downy, red-bellied, and ladder-backed woodpeckers. You may well hear a wild turkey calling while you gaze at the tame swans, ducks, and geese that call the ponds home. Hummingbirds may be ruby-throated or black-chinned.

Sponsored Activities: Many events, including festivals and concerts, as well as workshops are held on site. Pick up a current schedule or call for information.

Tour and Rental Policies: Tours are self-guided, with an excellent map and good signage making it easy to overload on information. If you want an expert-guided tour, that can be arranged for groups of no more than 12, but the fee is a hefty $100.

Facilities for weddings could not be more elegant. Choose your venue from a formal brick Channel Garden with large pavilions, an intimate chapel complete with antique bell, or a wooden pavilion overlooking a lovely lake. Changing rooms and kitchen facilities are available, too. Whichever location you choose will be blessed with fragrance and bloom. You'll need reservations at least three months in advance. Call 940-682-4856.

Volunteer and Support Opportunities: Membership is only $30 a year, and it's a bargain, since it gets you into the garden free anytime you want to go, provides discounts on workshops and plant sales, and includes a newsletter. The whole family can be included for $100. If you're willing to work for garden privileges, consider volunteering. For a minimum of eight hours a month as a volunteer, you get unlimited access to the garden, ten passes for friends or family, discounts on plants, and a neat T-shirt.

Driving Instructions: From Mineral Wells, drive about five miles east on Highway 180. Turn north (left) onto Maddux Road. Or, from Weatherford, take U.S. Highway 180 west. Watch for

Maddux Road on the right as you near Mineral Wells. Turn north (right) and take off through the scrub and wildflowers. You'll soon come to a beautiful brick and stone entry on the right, with a sign that proclaims Clark Gardens and shows off a four-foot diameter steel iris blossom.

"A lot of people thought we could only produce cactus in West Texas."

Kenneth Landon, Director, International Water Lily Collection

San Angelo

San Angelo City Parks and International Water Lily Collection

San Angelo Chamber of Commerce
500 Rio Concho Drive
San Angelo, Texas 76903
915-653-1206; 800-375-1206
Park Headquarters: 915-657-4279
email: info@sanangelotexas.org
http://www.sanangelotexas.org

Fee: Free.

Accessibility: Varies; call for details.

Days and Hours: Open daily.

Garden Type: Civic gardens in public parks.

Garden Size: Varies.

Themes and Special Features: A tiny water garden tucked into a quiet city park in the very heart of Texas is probably the most prestigious garden in the state. Internationally recognized as holding one of the most important water lily collections in the world, this tranquil spot is also home to birds, dragonflies, butterflies, and roses and a host of other colorful plantings.

The Gardens: San Angelo is a city of gardens, each small but distinctive. Civic League Park at Beauregard and Park Street is home to the International Water Lily Garden and Municipal Rose Garden. Up to 150 species of water lilies may be on view at any one time, and some of them are almost always blooming, at least from mid-April to early October. Best time of the day to catch them flowering is probably between 10:00 A.M. and 2:30 P.M.

The one lily everyone wants to see is the Victoria, "the world's largest water lily," whose pad may reach eight feet in diameter. Other, less showy species may be rarer and even endangered except for their preservation in gardens like this one. Some can no longer be found in the wild at all. Five species of water lilies are native to Texas, and all are represented here. Some, like the Victorias, bloom only at night, but special lighting has been installed to permit you to see them then.

When you leave the Lily Garden, take a stroll through the Rose Garden. It's quite extensive and well signed. Together, the lily and rose gardens make up a truly exquisite scene that packs a lot of punch for its size.

In Rio Concho Park, in the 400 and 500 blocks of Rio Concho Drive, you will find a gazebo, a popular wedding site, and colorful beds of flowers, cacti, roses, and other perennials and annuals. The Sunken Garden at South Abe Street and West Avenue D holds a canna lily garden boasting what may be the largest number of cultivars in any public garden in the country. What a sight this is in full bloom!

A four-mile walking path follows the North Concho River through several parks. Footbridges, antique lighting fixtures, fountains, gardens, and a golf course make this a pleasant walk.

Don't-Miss Feature: A charming water feature on a wall near the lily garden spouts a trickle of water for birds to frolic in. Sit awhile and enjoy their antics.

Bird Alert: In the wooded parks you may find eastern Phoebe, yellow-billed cuckoo, or summer tanager. Western kingbird nests in the Sunken Garden. The hummingbird will probably be black-chinned.

Tour Policy: Tours are self-guided, unless you can call two weeks ahead. Group tours can be set up for a minimal fee.

Support and Volunteer Opportunities: The city of San Angelo pays for the upkeep of the gardens, but volunteers with the Concho Valley Master Gardener Association and the San Angelo Council of Garden Clubs have a hand in it, too, as do other private sponsors.

Driving Instructions: The Civic League Park is almost downtown, west of U.S. Highway 87 and west of the Concho River. Look for it at the intersection of West Beauregard and Park Drive. The Sunken Garden with the canna collection is about a mile south of there at West Avenue D and South Abe Street. Rio Concho Park is east of U.S. 87 on Rio Concho Drive. If you get lost, holler for help: 915-653-1206.

Finding More Gardens in West Texas

Abilene

McMurry College has a lovely iris garden near the intersection of 16th and Sayles Streets that offers a special treat in early spring.

Amarillo

Ogallala Water Gardeners host a tour of water gardens in private homes in July. Contact the club at the Amarillo Botanical Gardens, 806-352-6513, or pick up information at any area nursery where water gardening supplies are sold.

Lubbock

Two tours of private gardens are sponsored by the Lubbock Memorial Garden, one in the spring visiting home gardens, one in the late summer taking in water gardens. Call 806-797-4520 for this year's details.

A visitor to West Texas once asked, "Does it ever rain out here?"

"Yep," replied the rancher. "Remember in the Bible where it rained for 40 days and 40 nights?"

The visitor said, "Oh, Yes. Noah's flood."

"Well," the rancher said with quiet pride, "we got almost two and a half inches of that."

Appendix A

The Author's Texas Gardens Awards

1. Most exuberant: The Antique Rose Emporium in Independence
2. Best example of Less Is More: The Japanese Garden in Fort Worth Botanic Garden
3. Most passionate: The Sunken Garden in San Antonio
4. Best four-season display: The Dallas Arboretum and Botanical Garden
5. Biggest bang for the bucks: Clark's Gardens in Mineral Wells
6. Most jewel-like: Kumamoto En, the Japanese Garden inside the San Antonio Botanical Garden
7. Most flamboyant: The Azalea and Spring Flower Trail in Tyler each spring
8. Most prestigious: The International Water Lily Collection in San Angelo
9. Most formal: The Gardens at Bayou Bend in Houston
10. Most unique personality: Chandor Gardens in Weatherford
11. Prettiest hybrid-tea roses: Memorial Rose Garden in Victoria (also wins award for Quietest)

12. Most moving memorial: Cashion Memorial Garden at TAMU in Bryan-College Station
13. Cutest Children's Garden: The Beatrix Potter Garden at The Antique Rose Emporium in Independence
14. Best outdoor classroom: A tie between SFA Mast Arboretum in Nacogdoches and Chihuahuan Desert Gardens of the Centennial Museum at the University of Texas at El Paso.
15. Most unexpected: The Herb Garden at the Limpia Hotel in Fort Davis
16. Best bet for basil: Pure Luck Organics in Dripping Springs
17. The only one in Texas: Shakespeare Garden in Kilgore
18. Most neighborly: A tie between Zilker Botanic Garden in Austin and Fort Worth Botanic Gardens
19. Best Butterfly Ranch: The Fredericksburg Butterfly Ranch in Fredericksburg
20. Best Butterfly Garden: Texas Discovery Gardens in Dallas
21. Best Herb Garden: The Natural Gardener in Austin
22. Largest public rose garden in the USA, maybe in the whole world: Tyler Municipal Rose Garden

Appendix B

A Dozen Don't-Miss Gardens for Rose Lovers

1. The Antique Rose Emporium in Independence
2. Memorial Rose Garden in Victoria
3. Fort Worth Botanic Garden Rose Ramp and Oval
4. Tyler Municipal Rose Garden
5. TAMU Horticulture Center in Bryan-College Station
6. El Paso Rose Garden
7. San Angelo Municipal Park Rose Garden
8. Beaumont Botanic Gardens
9. San Antonio Botanical Garden
10. Clark Gardens in Mineral Wells
11. Stroud Memorial Rose Garden in Houston's Hermann Park
12. Lubbock Memorial Arboretum

Appendix C

Six Gardens with Great Conservatories for Tropical Plants

1. Beaumont Botanic Gardens
2. Corpus Christi Botanical Gardens
3. Texas Discovery Gardens in Dallas
4. Fort Worth Botanic Garden
5. Moody Gardens Rain Forest in Galveston
6. San Antonio Botanic Garden

Appendix D

Some Gardens by Theme

Azalea Extravaganzas

Austin: Memorial Azalea Garden in Zilker Botanic Garden
Beaumont: McFaddin-Ward House
Dallas: Arboretum
Houston: Gardens at Bayou Bend
Houston: River Oaks Garden Club Azalea Trail
Houston/Humble: Mercer Arboretum and Botanic Garden
Jefferson: Spring Walking Tours
Marshall: Starr Family State Historical Park
Mineral Wells: Clark Gardens
Nacogdoches: The Ruby M. Mize Azalea Garden
Nacogdoches: Stephen F. Austin Mast Arboretum
Tyler: Azalea and Spring Flower Trail
Tyler: Breedlove Nursery

Butterfly Gardens

Austin: The Natural Gardener
Austin: Zilker Botanic Garden
Dallas: Texas Discovery Gardens
Fredericksburg: Butterfly Ranch and Habitat
Galveston: Moody Gardens Rain Forest
Houston: Cockrell Butterfly Center
Kerrville: Riverside Nature Center
San Antonio: Botanical Garden
Weslaco: Valley Nature Center

Cactus Gardens

Alamo: Sunderland's Cactus Garden
Alpine: Sul Ross State University Cactus Garden
Austin: Zilker Botanic Garden
El Paso: Chihuahuan Desert Gardens of the Centennial Museum at UTEP
El Paso: TAMU Research Center
Fort Davis: Chihuahuan Desert Research Institute and Visitor Center
Fort Worth: Botanic Garden
Hale Center: Bell Park Cacti Garden
Harwood: Kactus Korral
Lajitas-Terlingua: Barton Warnock Environmental Education Center
Weslaco: Valley Nature Center

Children's Gardens

Bryan/College Station: Texas A&M University Horticultural Gardens
Chandler: Blue Moon Gardens
Corpus Christi: Botanical Gardens
Dallas: Arboretum
Houston: Topiary Garden at Bayou Bend
Independence: Antique Rose Emporium
Mineral Wells: Clark Gardens
San Antonio: Botanical Garden
Waco: The Earle-Harrison House and Gardens on Fifth Street

Cottage Gardens

Austin: Mayfield Park Garden
Chandler: Blue Moon Gardens
Fort Worth: Weston Gardens in Bloom
Independence: Antique Rose Emporium
Lampasas: Hickory Hill Herbs and Antique Roses

San Antonio: Schultze House Cottage Garden
Sherman: Texoma Landscapes
Whitewright: Old Rose Tour in May

Daffodil Meadow

Gladewater: Mrs. Helen Lee's Daffodil Garden

Daylily Displays

Alvin, Austin, Dallas, Pearland, San Antonio: American
Hemerocallis Display Gardens
Amarillo: Botanical Gardens
Houston: Mercer Arboretum
Mineral Wells: Clark Gardens
Paris: Pine Branch Daylily Garden
Orange: Pinehurst Garden

Estate Gardens

Beaumont: McFaddin-Ward House
Houston: Gardens at Bayou Bend
Marshall: Starr Family State Historical Park
San Antonio: McNay Art Museum
Tyler: Breedlove Nursery
Waco: Earle-Harrison House
Weatherford: Chandor Gardens

Fragrance (Sensory) Gardens

Amarillo: Botanical Gardens
Austin: Zilker Botanic Gardens
Beaumont: Botanical Gardens

El Paso: Chihuahuan Desert Gardens of the Centennial Museum at UTEP
Houston: Garden Center
Lubbock: Memorial Arboretum
San Antonio: Botanical Garden

Herb Gardens

Athens: East Texas Arboretum
Austin: The Natural Gardener
Austin: It's About Thyme
Bryan-College Station: Cashion Memorial Garden at TAMU
Dallas: Arboretum
Dripping Springs: Pure Luck Organics
Fort Davis: The Limpia Hotel
Fredericksburg: Herb Farm
Independence: The Antique Rose Emporium
Kilgore: Texas Shakespeare Garden
Lampasas: Hickory Hill Herbs
Mineral Wells: Clark Gardens
Roundtop: McAshan Gardens at Festival Hill
San Antonio: Botanical Garden
San Antonio: Schultze House
Waco: Heritage Homestead

Hummingbird Gardens

Aransas Pass: Newbury Park Hummingbird Garden
Rockport-Fulton: Rockport Demonstration Bird Garden
Rockport-Fulton: Annual Hummer/Bird Celebration

Japanese Gardens

Austin: Zilker Botanic Garden
Beaumont: Botanical Gardens
Fort Worth: Japanese Garden
Fredericksburg: Japanese Garden of Peace
Houston: Japanese Garden at Hermann Park
Lubbock: Memorial Arboretum
San Antonio: Botanical Garden
San Antonio: Sunken Garden
Weatherford: Chandor Gardens (Chinese)

Orchid Collection

Corpus Christi: Botanical Gardens

Poinsettias

Brenham: Ellison's Greenhouses
McAllen: Poinsettia Celebration
McKinney: Crump's Gardens

Rare and Endangered Plants

Alamo: Sunderland's Cactus Garden
El Paso: Chihuahuan Desert Gardens of the Centennial Museum at UTEP
El Paso: TAMU Research Center
Fort Davis: Chihuahuan Desert Research Institute and Visitor Center
Hempstead: Peckerwood Garden, Yucca Do Nursery
Houston/Humble: Mercer Arboretum
Lajitas-Terlingua: Barton Warnock Environmental Education Center
San Angelo: International Water Lily Collection

Shakespeare Garden

Kilgore: Texas Shakespeare Garden

Water Lily Collections

Brookshire: Lilypons Water Gardens
San Angelo: International Water Lily Collection

Wildflowers

Austin: Lady Bird Johnson Wildflower Center
Fredericksburg: Wildseed Farms
McKinney: Heard Natural Science Museum Native Plant Garden
San Antonio: Botanical Garden
(You will find native plants in most of the gardens mentioned in this book.)

Xeric Gardens

Alpine: Sul Ross State University Cactus Garden
Austin: Lady Bird Johnson Wildflower Center
Austin: Zilker Botanical Garden
Bryan/College Station: Texas A&M University Horticultural Gardens
El Paso: Chihuahuan Desert Gardens of the Centennial Museum at UTEP
El Paso: Texas A&M Agricultural Research and Extension Center
Fort Davis: Chihuahuan Desert Research Institute and Visitor Center
Fort Worth: Weston Gardens in Bloom
Kerrville: Riverside Nature Center
Houston/Humble: Mercer Arboretum
Lajitas-Terlingua: Barton Warnock Environmental Education Center
McAllen: Lower Rio Grande Valley Botanical Gardens and Nature Center

McKinney: Heard Natural Science Museum Native Plant Garden
Mineral Wells: Clark Gardens
Nacogdoches: Stephen F. Austin University Mast Arboretum
San Antonio: Botanical Garden
San Antonio: Schultze House
Weslaco: Valley Nature Center

Index of Gardens